Enrique X. de Anda Alanís

FÉLIX CANDELA

TASCHEN

HONG KONG KÖLN LONDON LOS ANGELES MADRID PARIS TOKYO

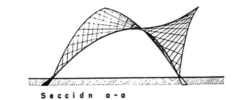

Seccion a-a

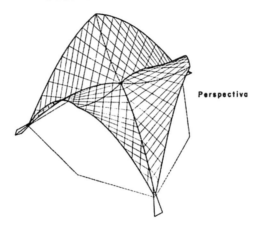

Perspectiva

Illustration page 2 ▶ *Los Manantiales* Restaurant,
under construction, Xochimilco, Mexico City,
1957
Illustration page 4 ▶ Design of the San José Hotel
Casino in Puerto Rico
© 2008 TASCHEN GmbH
Hohenzollernring 53, D-50672 Köln
www.taschen.com

Editor ▶ Peter Gössel, Bremen
Project management ▶ Katrin Schumann, Bremen
Design and layout ▶ Gössel und Partner, Bremen
Editorial coordination ▶ Sonja Altmeppen/Agentur
für Bildschöne Bücher, Berlin
Translation ▶ Karl E. Johnson, Berlin
Proofreading ▶ Michele Tilgner, Gröbenzell

Printed in Germany
ISBN: 978-3-8228-3724-5

To stay informed about upcoming TASCHEN
titles, please request our magazine at
www.taschen.com/magazine or write to
TASCHEN America, 6671 Sunset Boulevard,
Suite 1508, USA-Los Angeles, CA 90028,
contact-us@taschen.com, Fax: +1-323-463.4442.
We will be happy to send you a free copy of
our magazine which is filled with information
about all of our books.

Contents

Introduction

Opposite page:
Church of Our Miraculous Lady, Mexico City,
1953

Born at the start of the twentieth century, Félix Candela worked in the field of architecture between 1940 and 1997, the year of his death. In the history of modern architecture, Candela is considered the creator of a construction system whose two distinguishing features were typical of the twentieth-century world: the use of reinforced concrete and defining architectural space in connection with the fourth dimension of time. But who was this *hidalgo*, or nobleman, who never lost his Madrid accent after living thirty years in Mexico, and who made himself directly responsible for the design and the construction of nearly ten million square feet of remodeled space?

It was said that Candela belonged to a group of architects who, from the 1950s onward, used concrete membranes to create vast spaces with monumental geometric forms and included Eero Saarinen, Oscar Niemeyer, and Jørn Utzon. Yet only a glance at Candela's writings—especially those in which he refers to his architecture's structural and formal qualities—shows how wrong it is to consider him part of this group. In fact, he protested against being associated with the formal intentions of these men. Candela's approach was very clear: even if his structures suggested lofty, creatively daring design fantasies, their construction always demonstrated a clear shift from geometry to the realization of the structures in space. His forms unfolded in space, developed from figures and surfaces, and respected a mathematical and construction principle in which points, parallels, and sections formed an abiding law. Candela's criticism of his contemporaries' concrete-membrane designs was based on the argument that they evolved purely from a gesture of their creator's will. His caustic reaction to the roof shells of the Sydney Opera House, for example, makes the position he took easy to recognize: these membranes could only have been produced thanks to structural solutions by Ove Arup, since the roof shells designed by Jørn Utzon failed to satisfy the necessary organic requirements for achieving stability through their form alone.

Candela was born on January 27, 1910 in Madrid, where he studied at the Escuela Superior de Arquitectura and graduated in 1935. Describing how his career began, he said: "I came to study architecture by coincidence, without the slightest belief in my abilities as an artist or a designer. It might have been the enormous uncertainty on my part that led me toward technical matters and materials [...] mathematics and structures [...]." In June of 1939, after serving in the Spanish Civil War as an engineer and officer of the Republicans, and following his internment as a political prisoner in a concentration camp in Perpignan, Candela made his way to Mexico. In 1941 he obtained Mexican citizenship, started a family, taught himself civil engineering, and, as an autodidact, continued doing research into the area of mathematical sciences. His goal was to master the structural mechanics of area-covering frameworks. These first ten years in exile proved that choosing architecture as a profession was not the coincidence he first thought it was. He did, after all, have a strong inclination towards mathematics; he constantly used it to grasp constructional aspects of doubly-curved surfaces in space, to complete analyses, and to transfer the results to the concrete construction method. Without his passion for this subject, Candela would have been

merely an excellent mathematician and not the remarkable inventor of a formal system that allowed him to construct concrete membranes based on geometric shapes never seen before in such dimensions, nor visualized in space in this manner, endowed with aesthetic qualities conceived by the master himself and his coworkers.

In 1952, Candela's Cosmic Rays Pavilion was built on the campus of the Ciudad Universitaria of UNAM (Universidad Nacional Autónoma de México). As the first example of a roof-shell design created with a hyperbolic paraboloid (*hypar*), it marks the start of the most brilliant period of Candela's creative output. Over the next thirty years, he was responsible for 896 constructions. This corresponded to having two and a half structures per month designed and constructed under his supervision. In addition, there were 1,439 other projects, not all of which were realized. In 1971 Candela emigrated to the United States, opened an international consultancy, and retired from the construction of buildings. At the University of Illinois, he continued the full professorship started in Mexico. He died on December 7, 1997, in North Carolina.

Though always open to new ideas, Candela possessed a critical nature. His work completed in Mexico embodied two principles: creating architectural designs with spectacular forms and dimensions on the one hand, and employing a math-based

Experimental roof shell for the Raul Fernandez factory, San Bartolo, Mexico, 1950

Experimental roof shell for the Raul Fernandez factory, San Bartolo, Mexico, 1950
Perspective drawing

work method on the other. Defined by sections of geometric shapes, this method allowed him to construct forms able to unfold in space with great complexity. During an interview conducted on November 25, 1989, when asked where his architectural ambition came from when he started working in Mexico, Candela's temperamental response was simply: "That's easy. I wanted to construct things! Namely buildings!" Yet critics wondered whether to consider him an architect or an engineer. Although it was common in Mexico, during the years when Candela developed his best work, for architects to assume responsibility for the construction as well, based on the vast number of Candela's commissioned works and the peculiar stamp of their form, the criticism and specialists' committees of that period suggest that the core of Candela's functionality failed to coincide with the professional goals of architecture.

Starting with the advancements enabling the first steps toward the design of math-based concrete membranes, Félix E. Buschiazzo lists the most important achievements in the history of the concrete shell: in 1821 French mathematician Cauchy applies differential equations to the Elasticity Theory; in the late nineteenth century, Frenchmen Aimond and Laffaire develop the Hyperbolic Paraboloid Theory; from 1921 to 1923, in Orly, Eugène Freyssinet builds hangars for navigable airships and designs for them roof shells in the form of paraboloids; in 1939 Robert Maillart constructs the Zurich Exhibition Hall; in the late 1930s, in Madrid, Eduardo Torroja conceives the roof shell of the *Frontón de Recoletos* using cylindrical double arches; in 1948 Pier Luigi Nervi designs the Turin Exhibition Salon; in 1952 Félix Candela constructs the first hyperbolic paraboloid (Cosmic Rays Pavilion), whose crown thickness measures an average of 2 cm; and, in 1960, the same Candela roofs over the 580,000 square feet of the Bacardi & Co. Bottling Plant with 4 cm-thick cross vaults whose thrust and tension, exceeding the edges of their arches, are deflected to the ground on only twenty-four vault abutments.

Candela did not invent thin-shell construction, but he was the creator of membrane stress equations that made it possible to apply statistical processes to a structure's conception and conduct stress-confirming experiments on its form and thickness. With these equations, Candela could grasp and analyze the distribution of stress on

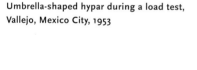

Umbrella-shaped hypar during a load test, Vallejo, Mexico City, 1953

Celestino Fernández factory warehouse,
Vallejo, Mexico City, 1955

shell structures and attain, as he put it, the "lightest possible results" without wasting materials. This procedure instilled his forms with grace and refinement. It was no secret that Candela's coworkers and partners could choose the geometric form they thought best suited the project. But the master always had the last word: "I took charge when it came time to determining the appropriate height [...]."

Candela insistently criticized the analytical procedures used by most engineers. In his opinion, these produced superfluous elements and faulty data. His own procedures developed from geometry (from the image of bodies revolving and intersecting in space) and produced forms already part of the geometric repertoire. According to the logic of geometry-based curvature combinations, figures such as these were capable of standing upright when constructed with materials that guaranteed their stability. This was where reinforced concrete and reinforced-steel mesh were applied. After ensuring the structure's stability, the second step was to calculate the exact extent and position of the structure's materials, and, by using only what was absolutely necessary, to minimize the material expenditure and weight. In this respect, Candela obtained dazzling results with his membrane-stress equations. While verifying the stress that structures were subjected to, they proposed balance-giving materials as well. The advent of rupture theories, emphasizing simple structural analysis and gravitational shifts on the qualities of building materials and their behavior, allowed him to further his understanding of load-distribution analysis as applied to thin-shell structures. When the number and nature of materials had to be confirmed, the master based his work on structural analysis; he avoided hypar-related statistics and focused on Rupture Theory. Unlike the German architects who compromised their shells' geometric forms with the amount of concrete used, Candela managed to produce thinner concrete shells with a thickness ranging from 2 to 5 cm.

Candela's "experimental" creative phase, for the later development of his most important projects, occurred at the start of the postwar period. This was when local architectural tendencies in Latin America had reached their maturity (in Argentina,

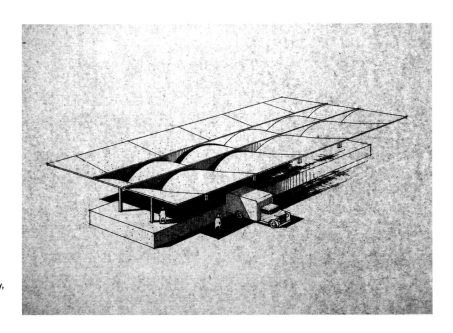

Roofed-over loading ramp of the Ceimsa dairy, Tlalnepantla, Mexico, 1952
Perspective drawing

Brazil, Mexico, and Venezuela), and when their structural qualities quickly gained recognition due to their originality and striking plasticity. The design qualities of these remarkable local constructions were not only indebted to the talents of Latin American architects such as Augusto H. Álvarez, Luís Barragán, Félix Candela, Lucio Costa, Enrique de Moral, Oscar Niemeyer, and others, but also to the fact that the needed means to create Mexico's infrastructure were now available. The industrialization of many countries at that time played a major role as well. Candela offered his structures to Mexico's industrial sector at a moment when he could count on support of the government with its economic consolidation. He had two "commodities" to offer: production speed and reduced material expenditure. Project by project—regardless of the complexity of a design—the economics of the system devised by Candela lowered construction costs. Aiding the industrial sector with the building of factories, plants, and warehouses placed Candela at the forefront of an area of production whose results were immediately visible. This prompted him to say (when Mexico's new civil engineering laws went into effect): "I've opened my umbrellas over half the country already!" This umbrella form, composed of a supporting foot and a four-sided concrete shell balanced above it, is the most famous of all the structural forms conceived by Candela. Constructing tens of thousands of square feet of such regularly ordered forms paved the way to the major works of his career. For Candela, his work in Mexico compared to managing a relaxed open-air laboratory that demanded novel ideas of all its scientists, because to a certain extent he always worked with life-size prototypes.

Félix Candela actively consolidated and disseminated his theories in the projects that he realized. He also published technical papers, essays, and critical studies on architectural practices, student education, and ecological issues. As a thinker with a cosmopolitan background, Candela taught at the university and knew exactly how to impart his wealth of ideas through lectures. His discourses were distinguished by at least three equally important features: the use of historical thinking as a way to understand and categorize architectural achievements of the past; a command of topics

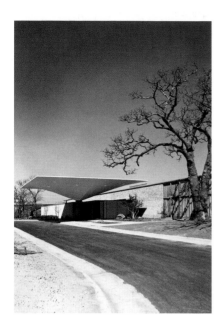

Crossroads Restaurant, Great Southwest
Industrial District, Texas, USA, 1958

related to math- and geometry-based reinforced-concrete forms in space; and an ongoing critique of current structural models, concepts of architecture (European functionalism and rationalism), and the faulty logic regarding the use of reinforced concrete and constructive-analysis systems. His intellectual work resembled that of European engineers of the late nineteenth century—personalities who used the potential of iron to bridge spaces over huge distances. Yet Candela's main tool was his intuition, which he used to discover new forms and innovative ways of applying concrete. These took neither the form of barrel vaulting, roofing for machinery halls of the World's Fair in France in the late nineteenth century, nor open floor plans with laterally arranged rows of columns, but rather reflected his deeper concern for "delicate and breathing forms suggestive of the fragile yet fleshy curves of a tropical bird, everything set in motion by a dazzling technology [...]" (Chueca Goitia). Also he greatly benefited from his sense of clarity: this allowed him to see, grasp, and utilize the abstract realm of mathematics to reach exact solutions and guarantee the stability of doubly-curved, vibrating forms.

Beginning in 1953 Candela held a professorship at what was then the *Escuela Nacional de Architectura* of the UNAM. In keeping with his professional experience, he taught a math course, another on geometry, and a third on "Material Sciences and Tensile Strength." Because of the complex manner of presenting the material covered in Candela's courses, it rarely happened that his lectures were fully attended. Still, it was a fact that the presence of this celebrity at the university—a man praised for his originality demonstrated between 1950 and 1970—added excitement to the learning experience. What remained more important than Candela's courses for the generation of students who made his acquaintance at the university was having his thinking documented: his lectures, interviews, and recorded discussions were often published in newspapers of the period. During a 1966 lecture given to professors of the Escuela de Architectura Candela described his concept for training architects: "Instead of nurturing unbridled imagination and inventiveness, we should impress upon our students an awareness of physical boundaries [...] The same architect who has no idea how a supporting beam works thinks himself qualified to create extraordinary structures." But, with both feet firmly planted on the ground, the architect who did know how to create extraordinarily beautiful buildings—structures practically afloat between the sky and bodies of water—never forgot that logic and simplicity are the guidelines of creativity.

In his essay *Divagaciones estructurales en torno al estilo* ("Structural Digressions on Style"), Candela emphasizes the significance he attaches to style and offers a step-by-step explanation and basic history of the role of concrete in defining the twentieth-century style. He opens with the comment: "[The solution] to the fundamental architectural problem of our time is the search for a style or mutual language capable of offering more than the unjustified boredom of everyday routine." He goes on to view style as a social "code" developed from a political and philosophical program, accepting how different stylistic types repeatedly take up symbols handed down through the centuries when, among other things, they form an "easily grasped and universally understood language." From his study of history, Candela concludes that he "admires the structural qualities of the Greek and Gothic styles," and that "our time" strongly resembles the "period prior to the birth of the Gothic," because of the artistic freedom that characterizes it and that made itself so evident in the first half of the twentieth century.

Candela discovered that he could—at least in part—modify a city's ambience, as demonstrated with churches, sculptures, and industrial plants. Also he realized that he could treat tens of thousands of square feet with a single element and, with repetition, develop an enormous roof shell whose sheer vibrating movement defied monotony and lent the site a new urban identity.

When asked about his interest in concrete shells, Candela explained that his work was primarily focused on establishing an agreement between the design and the analysis of reinforced concrete. In an interview on November 25, 1989, he explained: "We have different methods at our disposal for analyzing structures. I tried to simplify them so that I could find the one best suited to my own possibilities. What I did was formulate equations for analyzing stress factors in membranes." These equations made it necessary to alter all the analytical procedures used until then to master or control incurring stresses. What made this development so important for modern architecture was that, in the broadest sense, it replaced the old concept of a support-and-load relationship.

Let us take a moment to consider Candela's work in the functional area of three-dimensional load-bearing structures. This is, after all, the key to understanding the nature of his creativity and the course it took. From general to specific matters, his initial criticism was directed at how architects use concrete as a building material: they "imitate" load-bearing systems made of wood and steel without taking advantage of concrete's adaptability and flexibility, and this leads to the fatal cube-shaped block, a form that characterizes modern architecture. In this context, his criticism of specialized drawings by structural analysts stands out as well: far from offering architects any direction-giving support, the former seem obsessed with applying mathematical formulas, which guaranteed stability but also hindered innovative spatial perception. In my opinion, Candela's contribution to architectural space in the twentieth century is recognizable on three levels: firstly, his curved surfaces were not only constructed on the ideal foundation of mathematics, but were also actually built in the real world;

secondly, the equations he devised for analyzing the actual strength of materials, which were necessary to establish whether a concrete shell is rigid enough, replacing both the Elasticity Theory and the Warped Surfaces Analysis; thirdly, his idea to use wooden formwork, allowing him to transfer his imaginary figures in the space of virtually vibrating curves to a physical reality.

While the Cosmic Rays Pavilion was under construction, Candela had a working knowledge of geometry and mathematics, the areas from which his ideas evolved. The previous year, he had published his essay *Toward a New Philosophy of Structures*, in which he criticized the analyses of various specialists. He spoke of "incompetence and faulty logic in the calculation methods based on the Elasticity Theory," and rejected its use, arguing that it made no sense applying this theory to reinforced concrete, an inconsistent material in which steel would concentrate at certain points and result in erratic properties. Due to these points, Candela preferred to work with the Membrane Stress Theory, and it was for this theory that he invented equations allowing him to determine a material's resistance and behavior in space. After establishing the new theory (when he stopped relying on the hyper-statistical model), his activities no longer had to take into acount the irregularities that normally occurred in reinforced concrete. He based his work on structural formulas and—new in construction engineering then —his acquired knowledge of the effects of tangential stress and continual curvatures on concrete shells, whose geometric design guaranteed stability and long-lasting load-bearing functions. From this moment on, the term used to describe this type of spatial system would be "shell." In Candela's office, the essential tools of the trade for completing analyses were a slide rule and logarithm table. But, as reported by Juan Antonio Tonda, one of the master's students and coworkers, one could also rely on the help of a mathematician whose duties included solving Adolf Pucher's differential equations. A hand-operated Swedish calculating machine was in the adjacent studio, and, after punching out a decimal point, it completed an approximate four-digit calculation.

This brings us to Félix Candela's geometric repertoire. The starting point is formed by conical sections, including the parabolic, hyperbolic, and ellipse. The second step is transferring these shapes to the third dimension by executing a rotation and producing forms with principal curvatures running in the same direction, as with the paraboloid, hyperboloid, and ellipsoid (the group of standard surfaces). The third step, the translation process, produces surfaces running in opposite directions, the best known of these being the hyperbolic paraboloid (hypar), created by shifting one parabolic open at the bottom (a generator) along another open at the top and yielding a figure resembling a "saddle," a so-called saddle surface. At the time when Candela first showed an interest in continually curved façades and roof surfaces of concrete, these figures existed per definition already. But not until he discovered "the simplest of possible grade-two equations" did he make their construction possible by varying the thickness of the concrete and the amount of steel used to compensate for the structure's weight. The countless models of roof shells designed by Candela and his coworkers began as pieces of folded paper; these determined the shells' dimensions. Later, the paper models evolved into wooden formwork. Finally, what developed was a wealth of spatial and perceptual effects never known before in the repertoire of sensorial experiences of modern architecture.

Candela and his coworkers instinctively knew which type of geometric construction best suited the architectural task at hand. They could draft it on a piece of paper and,

Unrealized project: market building with numerous staggered vaults of different heights arranged on a cruciform plan, 1956

with networks of geometric lines, they rotated it to recognize its qualities, analyzed its material, and calculated how much of it to use to guarantee the structure's physical stability. At the end of these activities was another no less important process without which the structure could never have been built: engaging the creative and technical skills of masonry workers and carpenters. The first step was to apply by hand the ruled lines of paraboloids as a threadwork to the foundation, and later, with the help of wooden formwork, to make these unfold in midair, rotate, bend, fuse, and generate curves en route to forming complete geometric structures. What was visible on paper as the positions of axes and generators quickly developed in situ out of the material elements. Masonry workers applied iron-rod-bearing and wire-reinforced concrete to scaffolding erected by carpenters (Juan A. Tonda recalls Guadalupe Valencia and Lucio Jiménez) who had been in Candela's employ for years. No sooner had the structure been freed of the wooden supports, it was expected to assert itself in space and withstand every form of tensile stress to which concrete membranes are subjected.

Without being based on a particular theory, the spatial-dimensional nature of Candela's architecture echoes expressionism. In painting and music, we can say with relative certainty when stylistic descriptions of expressionism are apparent. But when this type of connection between author and reality shows itself in architecture, the topic forfeits some of its clarity and gives way to deception—especially when the conditions that have always characterized architecture are no longer clear. Yet Candela never entertained an artistic outlook along these lines. Here, too, his attitude was clear and unique: as options, he focused on forms in and of themselves and the intellectual

Design for a church

investigation leading to their design: "I believe that I'm a formalist because I see art as the will to create form, but always a well-ordered, harmonious, and stable form [...]." Besides Candela's already expressed opinions, there was another directed against rationalism in architecture: "One of the greatest absurdities of philosophical thinking is to insist that form is the inevitable consequence of analysis." Contrary to whatever one might think about Candela, imagining him working with his "slide rule" and calculating the curve of a paraboloid, he acknowledged that using one's intuition was the best way to design form. Candela's discourse had more to do with architectural forms than with space. It focused on the technical research that establishes an object's physical boundaries and contours in a landscape. He concerned himself with this, and it limited his architectural interest in constructional decoration: "I don't subscribe to the notion that we should happily throw ourselves into the arms of some baroque style of capricious and extravagant forms [...]." His explanation for becoming so involved with forms was that he hoped to define formalism "as a scientific investigation of spatial design without forgetting to include a detailed analysis of inner structure."

If we consider Candela's complete works, those numbered among his favorites (undoubtedly due to their aesthetic achievements), while keeping in mind attributes Joseph Casals ascribes to expressionist architecture, we see a correspondence regarding formal qualities. Casals points to the following qualities: a construction conceived as an organic whole; the vanishing of borders; a free-edged floor plan favoring free-flowing space; a sculptural modeling of exteriors; the emotional reactions of viewers;

and steep roof shells that practically reach the floor, making lateral walls and columns superfluous, almost eliminating them entirely.

Candela's coworkers (Manuel Larrosa, Guillermo Rosell de la Lama, Enrique de la Mora, Fernando López Carmona, Juan Antonio Tonda, Joaquín Álvarez Ordoñez, and others) were obliged to respect the deeper meaning always inherent of such collaborative endeavors. While the structure could have been conceived by any of them, it was always Candela who decided on its exact dimensions and proportions. Afterwards, however, the coworkers were needed to handle the refinement of structural details and to attain the best results within the realm of possibilities. They were also responsible for other construction tasks: installation, carpentry work, and decorative elements. The projects were realized in a genuine collaboration, with each participant delegated his or her responsibilities; had anyone in the team failed to do their job well, these projects would hardly have been granted the aesthetic qualities we admire them for today.

The last work completed in Mexico, the design and management of which Félix Candela oversaw, was the Olympic Sports Complex, built to accommodate the basketball championships of the 1968 Olympic Games in Mexico. Three years later, in 1971, Candela emigrated to the United States. He settled in Chicago, opened an international technical consultancy, and devoted a portion of his time to teaching. His leaving Mexico remained so controversial a topic because he never worked as an architect again. *Cubiertas Ala, S. A.*, the family business for which he constructed some 896 buildings with standardized area-covering structural elements, closed its doors in 1969. At the age of sixty-one, Candela was at the height of his career. His creative achievements had won for him a fame beyond Mexico's boarders. He had been honored in many countries with commissions and awards, and invited to lecture on his work. All this suggested that he would further develop his professional activities, search for new solutions, expand on his research in the field of mathematics, and oversee the construction of innovative roof shells. Instead, all this waited in vain for the architect's attention. It was his abrupt abandoning of a career characterized by so many contributions to a discourse on architectural space worldwide that made Candela's departure from the field so hard to grasp. This can be understood in no other way except as a traumatic, personal situation caused by a lack of commissions, and surely by a lack of professional recognition on the part of his colleagues.

It is possible that the number of commissions fell due to the rising cost of wood, which was, after all, the most important material for building formwork. In spite of this, in 1989, Félix Candela and Fernando López Carmona, a coworker who participated in many projects, proudly stated that, per constructed square foot, building with steel-reinforced concrete was still very economical. In 1994, nearing the end of his life, Candela remarked: "I never searched for fame in Mexico where it was impossible to find, since no one puts their faith in you where you live; I searched for it abroad, where people began to write about me."

Because the building industry was completely different in the United States, it was impossible for Candela to fall back on his activities in Mexico as an architect or creator of projects and structural designs, and continue working as a project manager. In spite of this, he moved to Chicago and divided his time between teaching at the University of Illinois and offering professional advice to field-related colleagues commissioned with designing large-scale sports facilities. Owing to this new work

Oceanografic, **City of Arts and Sciences, Valencia, Spain, 1997**

situation, Candela had to go without certain key experiences: directing the unfolding geometric shapes down to the earth; establishing the project's physical guidelines and having these produce forms under the scaffolding; or witnessing the majestic unfolding of a roof shell: that special moment when the earth accepts the weight of the concrete at precisely those points where the structure is anchored, precisely where the master wanted the stress deflected.

Around 1980 Candela accepted work in Spain, which he undertook parallel to his North American activities. He was asked to collaborate on designing structures as well. This period not only witnessed Candela's retrospective in Madrid (1994), but also his professional liaison with Santiago Calatrava, who saw in him the giant that Isaac Newton spoke of and recognized the vast horizons spreading out behind Candela's shoulders: "A few of my projects, especially the early ones, were created solely out of admiration for Félix Candela's work [...]." Further proof of the professional affinity between the two architects was Candela's posthumous work. Calatrava had invited Candela to participate in the project Ciudad de las Artes y las Ciencias en Valencia (City of Arts and Sciences in Valencia, Spain). Inaugurated in 1998, this was one of Valencia's most important architectural enterprises during the final years of the twentieth century. Apart from proposals concerning the general structural criteria, Candela was asked to oversee the Valencia *Oceanografic* project. Basically, this involved a theme park consisting of a large aquarium and a series of installations distributed throughout the City of Valencia. The project was intended to draw visitors not only to the city's museums, but also to its auditoriums and exhibition spaces. The facility officially opened in 2002, five years after Candela's death.

For the water park, Candela designed installations for a one-million-square-foot complex that included an aquarium capable of holding over ten million gallons of salt water. The exhibition area's eleven towers are divided into above- and below-ground-level zones. Looming over the surface of the water, the *Oceanografic* houses in one of its cross vaults a restaurant resembling *Los Manantiales*. The façade of the main building's entrance features a huge hypar consisting of a large glass surface. Although the structure's design corresponded with Candela's methodical thinking, the height and width of the façades' hypar-parabolas are no longer as sublime as those in Xochimilco. Still, in the park's exhibition area focused on the Mediterranean, the Madrid-born master's concrete water lilies continue to coexist with Calatrava's dinosaur-like structures even today. This not only demonstrates the extent to which Candela's thinking has survived, but also the wide range of possibilities still at the disposal of eternal geometry, allowing it to stage more scenes in which fascinating forms unfold and unprecedented spaces emerge.

1951–1952 ▸ Cosmic Rays Pavilion
Ciudad Universitaria (University City), Mexico City
Collaborating Architect: Jorge González Reyna

Opposite page:
Staircase in its original state

Exterior in its present state

This small single-story structure with an area of almost 1,400 square feet was designed and built by Candela in the Ciudad Universitaria of the UNAM (Universidad Nacional Autónoma de México). Here the campus architecture faithfully exemplifies the International Style that was considered to be the path to modernism in Mexico in the 1940s. For this very reason, however, the pavilion's form perplexes. Its organic design visually opposes the dominating geometry of the surrounding university buildings, displaying colorful volumes, light-admitting façades, and reinforced-concrete frames. Not only do the curves of the pavilion's roof shell and supports stand in constant contrast to the colorful spectacle of the glimmering, transparent façades, the same applies to its shady ground-floor level. For all that, this structure—the first model not constructed purely as a prototype by Candela—earned the architect considerable international acclaim.

The architectural task involved developing a stable roof membrane as protection for a device used to measure neutrons. But the membrane had to be thin enough to allow cosmic rays to pass through it. So the structure's sole function was that of a container for a device at a specific location without the need for additional spaces. By the end of the 1940s, Candela had already completed several projects that proposed new ways of using geometry and pointed to a more dependable method of handling shell construction. As a result, Carlos Lazo, director of construction of the University City, commissioned Candela to construct a roof shell made of concrete, stipulating that it be, if possible, only 1 cm thick. In Candela's solution to the problem, the previous projects' cylindrical vaults were replaced by two hyperbolic paraboloids and mounted

21

The bordering wall originally running under the structure was partially demolished.

Section

on three parabolic arches. The thickness of the concrete at the curve of the shell's crown measured 2 cm. In 1995 Candela recalled that "[...] the project contributed to producing the thinnest highly durable shell membrane." Today the building is fifty-five years old and still boasts an intact structure. Although it serves a different purpose now, it still provides a contrast to the other buildings on the campus thanks to those qualities that Casals associates with expressionist architecture: it is both "astonishing and unexpected."

With the aesthetic line modulation of the doubly-curved concrete shell, which forms the basic structure, Candela was able to achieve a solution endowed with compelling three-dimensional force. On the ground level, three parabolic-shaped arches rise up with protruding supports. The upper portion of the arches serves as the structural framework of the laboratory, and the encompassing concrete membrane seems to rest in place above it without being anchored to the ground. The beauty of the design's three-dimensionality emerges directly from its cleverly devised proportions. As thin discs with well-balanced pressure and stress points, the arches do not seem to dominate the design: in light of the lateral bearing areas, the former seem to function like supports on the one hand and, because of their parabolic shape, convey a sense of elasticity on the other. The form and disposition of both corrugated gable-end surfaces contribute to an expression of monumentality, if on a smaller scale than the other campus buildings, characterized by their compactness and size.

Candela always thought highly of his solution with the gable surfaces. While not functioning as roof supports, they were still capable of assuming every possible role outside the structural complex, and their corrugated surfaces gave rise to a lively interplay of light and shadow, especially the south-facing surface. Nowhere—except on the stairs—do straight lines appear. The unusual aspect of the architecture lies in the self-confident manner in which the language of the curve is incorporated into a work of modern architecture—not as a contrast, but rather as an integral element. Candela completed this structure with great care and gave his attention to every detail: from the membrane's thickness and the height of the parabolic-shaped gable surfaces to the proportions of the arches and the interplay of light and dark waves.

In 1945 Candela published an essay entitled *Divagaciones estructurales en torno al estilo* ("Structural Digressions on Style") in which he addressed a topic that had preoccupied him for a long time: the difference between the role of the architect, responsible for the invention of form—viewed by cultural history since time immemorial as equaling architecture in and of itself—and the role of the engineer, the person concerned with the mechanics of materials, statistical factors, technical possibilities of the materials, and construction systems. The article adopts a conciliatory tone when its author suggests that formulating the "style" of the 1950s should be developed exclusively from the supporting concrete structure. Here Candela firmly emphasizes that the structural factor has long ceased to be used in the search for new forms, underscoring his personal theory of new architecture: "Essentially, efficient structural function depends on form." The Cosmic Rays Pavilion exemplifies this idea: while the form supplies the structural capacity, the entire structure is composed of its own supports. In 1955, in a critical text on the buildings of the architecturally structured part of the University City campus, Candela wrote: "The obsession with murals is justified by the intention somehow to compensate for the almost complete lack of expression in the contemporary architecture found here."

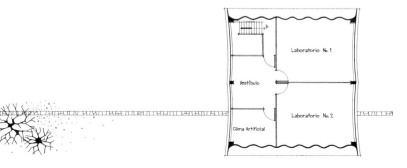

Site plan

1952 ▸ Chemical Sciences Auditorium

Ciudad Universitaria (University City), Mexico City
Collaborating Architects: Enrique Yáñez, Guillermo Rosell and Enrique Guerrero

Illustration of the distinctive cone shapes

Right:
Chemical Sciences Auditorium, 1952

Interior of both auditoriums

Opposite page:
Exterior as it appears today

In the eastern section of the University City campus, separate from the group of assembly halls and located in a garden complex, this building, too, was erected on the grounds of the Natural Sciences faculty. Architecturally, the intention was to create a division between the auditoriums and the academic complex in order to use them separately when necessary for important events. This special "sectioning-off" function inspired a three-dimensional design that stood out from the rest of the buildings. Interesting to note here is that Enrique Yáñez, chief architect of the design team of the Chemistry faculty, was among the forerunners of rationalism in Mexico.

This was one of the few instances in which Candela merely designed the structural plan without being directly involved in the construction. The project included two connecting buildings whose walls were built using a locally available natural stone—a material that was the architectural "hallmark" of all the buildings on the campus. In the case of the auditoriums, the stone was combined with a gray-toned mortar mixture, from which the building's impressive structural completion scarcely benefited. The task would have probably been better resolved in Candela's hands. The roof's concrete shell is composed of two truncated cones joined along a common edge. This was also the only time Candela used this particular shape, which embodied the full meaning of the building while providing an unlimited repertoire of geometric forms. The diameters of the cones range from 26 to 52 feet, and the vertical walls are stabilized by inclined supports of prestressed concrete, which stand removed from the structure of the roof.

1954 ▸ *La Jacaranda* Nightclub
Mexico City
Collaborating Architect: Max Borges, Jr.

Opposite page:
Formwork assembly

This now demolished nightclub, originally capped with a reinforced-concrete roof shell, was built in a district of Mexico City that was extremely fashionable in the 1950s because of its many galleries, restaurants, and bars. Interestingly, the building's structure reflected two phenomena: Candela's unquenchable desire to create a wide range of designs with his shells on the one hand, and the first attempts to revitalize an urban space with architectural structures removed from the geometric and formal language of rationalism on the other. The client wanted to create a restaurant (with a dance floor in a garden) whose prominent symbol would be a jacaranda tree—after which the nightclub was later named. Since establishments of this type were usually integrated into hotels, building such a club on its own was rarely considered in Mexico City. Also interesting is the fact that the nightclub's design is similar to the "dance hall" Oscar Niemeyer created ten years previously, on the shores of Pampulha Lake in Belo Horizonte, Brazil.

The semicircular ground plan accommodated the restaurant and dance floor. The sanitary facilities, bar, and kitchen were grouped around the outer edge. The structure's form was that of a quarter of a sphere and was linked with the garden complex via two openings: one was created by a cone shape penetrating the sphere, under which the so-called wishing well was located, and another by a hypar that opened onto an artificial waterfall. The shell's glazed façade allowed for an unobstructed view of the jacaranda tree at the front of the building. Since the nightclub was painted black, it remained virtually invisible at night.

Together with the dome of the Centro Gallego, built roughly the same year, this structure numbers among the only two concrete shells Candela ever constructed whose curves run in opposite directions. The reason for this might have been the exorbitant construction costs. With a spherical or elliptical surface like the one used for *La Jacaranda* nightclub, the formwork made of wooden boards and wedges had to be cut to different lengths and arranged parallel to one another in order for the applied concrete to produce a spherical form. Yet the wood for the "staves" was not reusable. Also their manufacture was far more time-consuming than the commonly employed method of constructing hypars. The difference in scaffolding for forms whose curvatures ran in the same direction was that the wooden boards extended beyond the supports and these could, in fact, be used repeatedly. While the wood dictated the form of the concrete surface, it conformed to the shape of the hypar.

Site plan

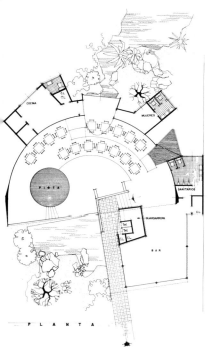

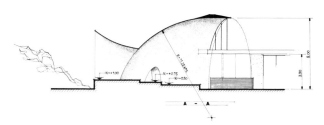

Cross-section

1952–1954 ▸ Customs Administration Warehouses

Vallejo Industrial District, Mexico City
Architectural Design: Carlos Recamier

Opposite page:
Photograph taken during construction

After the war, a medium-sized industrial district began to establish itself in the north of Mexico City and it developed rather successfully over the following years. Between 1950 and 1960, it was here that Candela constructed tens of thousands of square feet of concrete membranes using a construction plan based on statistical analysis methods. The relationship between client and architect was marked by the need to build systematically, quickly, and economically—requirements met by Candela's team: his troops of construction workers and each individual laborer. Colin Faber, a workshop coworker and author of the book *Candela: The Shell Builder*, described one of the more extreme cases: "A client could arrive in the morning carrying his rough site plans for a warehouse; the elevation plans would have to be drawn up that afternoon; and, like it happened once, the building contract would have to be signed that same evening."

In 1954 the Ministry of Finance commissioned Candela to build in this part of the city one of the most beautiful structures that he would ever create: the Customs Administration Warehouses for storing incoming merchandise for customs inspection. It comprised three laterally open halls in which delivery trucks were unloaded. The structure is composed of segments, each of which rests on four supports. Arranged in pairs, the rhombus-shaped supports or columns stand at a distance of 66 feet from one another and support the barrel-vaulted roof. On its sides, each support carries a protruding 20-foot-long side-wing whose vault reiterates the geometric curve of the middle barrel. Both side-wings are connected at the top by a horizontal suspension rod, which is attached to the crown of the main vault. The rhombus shape of the columns precisely corresponds to the diagram of the flexural stresses that act on it. Not unlike the form of the roof vaulting, the column was developed by means of a mathematically simulated trial-and-error process. The roof shell has a thickness of 4 cm, and those of the side-wings 5 cm. While the wings running along both sides of the building generate a coherent unity, the central vault between their segments leaves gaps for light to pass through. In its entirety, the complex perfectly illustrates Candela's work credo: select the simplest type of concrete shell load-bearing system and develop the beauty of its design through a meticulous handling of the details and the supports. In the Customs Administration Warehouses, the proportions of its few structural components—supports, vaults, suspension rods—and the refinement of its forms as well as the size of each element stand in a clear relationship to each other and they impart great elegance to the entire structure. This is a rare quality in warehouse construction. Years later, Colin Faber averred: "Some of Candela's warehouses are as beautiful as churches."

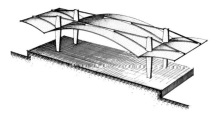

Perspective drawing

1953–1955 ▸ Church of Our Miraculous Lady

Narvarte, Mexico City

Opposite page:
Interior view

Photograph taken during construction

This church is both a landmark of modern international architecture and a huge success for its creator. Designed by Candela himself, this masterpiece made of sloped concrete surfaces was more like an experimental laboratory for the numerous spatial possibilities he was able to develop from the geometry of hypars. In a residential district of Mexico City, on a rectangular corner plot with a north-to-south principal axis, the structure built on this site had an entrance facing south and occupied almost the entire piece of property measering 93 x 159 feet. It commences with a small recessed narthex meant to keep the façade from merging with the front line of the neighboring building. Its eastern flank begins as a side aisle in front of the chapel. In a westerly direction the church is opened by two rows of four sloped columns. The design does not feature a crossing, but instead the impressive and airy space of the presbytery, resulting from the structure's sheer height and intensified incidence of light.

Juan Antonio Tonda, Candela's coworker during the design phase of the church, reports that twenty-one different types of hypar were used here, and that those of the central church nave were so severely angled that, during the analysis, the resulting

View from lateral nave in the central space
with the altar

Below:
Design of longitudinal façade

vertical stress caused an unexpected upward surge toward the crest of the roof. This made it necessary to lend the areas where the row of hypar shells come together greater weight. In spite of this measure, the interior conveys a sense of utter weightlessness (like in a Gothic church), about which Richard Neutra is said to have claimed that, when inside the building, only four centimeters separate one from divinity. In the case of the Miraculous Lady, the construction engineers' ideas regarding pressure points and stress proved to be antiquated in an age of continual advancements: it turned out that the compressive loads failed to run vertically from the top of the structure to the floor—but also that the geometry of the doubled curvatures effectively reversed the incurring stress without endangering the building's stability.

When we consider how Candela's church came into being, what first come to mind are suspense-filled moments like the dismantling of the wooden scaffolding—or the moment when the entire concrete structure sits perfectly, articulates its form, asserts itself on its own, and correctly transfers its weight to the floor. We can almost imagine the excitement that Candela and his team must have felt after removing the formwork and supports, after studying the curved surfaces perfectly balanced on their sloped

Spiral staircase to choir loft
Each freely overhanging step supports a
stringboard segment.

Below:
Design drawing for the font

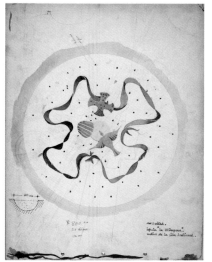

supports for the first time, and, while watching light filter through the church, darkening certain areas and brightening others, suddenly to notice the church's interior—almost lacking the space to unfold at all between so many unusual geometric shapes—begin to fill with dynamic ornamentation. Candela claimed that analysis merely justified the validity of the geometric plan. But his friend Ove Arup, one of the twentieth century's greatest minds in the field of Construction Analysis, thought otherwise: "Candela's designs develop from his strong sense of structure acquired from experience and corrected with approximate calculations. Later, he makes an exact analysis [...] In this way, employing his talent for making the right calculations, he gets quicker and better results than he would working with just a heap of mathematical equations."

The interior space of the "Miraculous Lady" is utterly unique. Nothing like it existed before. Candela himself could scarcely imagine its full impact. The space had enormous "expressionist" charisma, largely due to the sloped forms and innumerable light-and-dark effects (chiaroscuro) produced by its own surfaces. All this ran in remarkable contrast to the baroque American style in which spatial intensity is generated

through a coming forward of shapes and chiaroscuro effects. What makes this church so new and overwhelming is that never before were so many hypars constructed in one structure, and that, despite their widely varying curvatures, the result is a uniform spatial constellation. If we had to name the major steps that have led to advancements in contemporary architectural thinking, the knowledge and experience gained through the construction of this church would surely be one of them.

In addition, the three-dimensional quality of the light design and iconography, credited almost entirely to the architect José Luis Benlliure, should not be overlooked here. The light effects—whether produced through gaps, walls, shells, or polychrome glazing—are highly effective, and the Venetian-style mosaics and "angelic" religious figures are of the highest artistic quality.

View of two lateral altars

Below:
Longitudinal and cross-sections

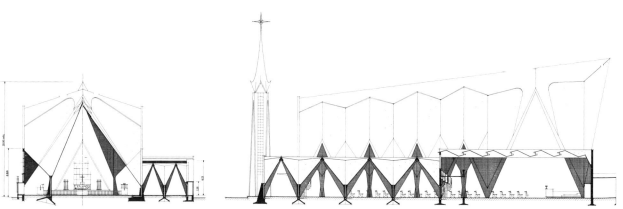

1955 ▸ Coyoacán Market

Coyoacán, Mexico City
Collaborating Architect: Pedro Ramírez Vázquez

A photograph of the "weightless" umbrellas, taken before the outer walls were erected

Coyoacán, a suburb in the south of Mexico City, dates back to the period of the Spanish viceroys. In the early 1950s, when the city administration had planned the construction of market halls as supply outlets for this region, Candela was asked to provide roofing whose supports would not hinder the crowds of people moving between the stalls. At that time families enjoyed buying their daily provisions at open-air markets whose roots reached back to the pre-Columbian period. These local markets, known as *tiangis*, traditionally consisted of individual stalls for sellers who protected themselves from inclement weather with material stretched over wooden frames, thus producing a tent-like structure called a *manta*. Like the market itself, these constructions had short life spans and were taken down at the end of the day.

Now the image of the city's old marketplace could be reestablished in the center of the newly constructed one, because the many rows of thin concrete sails (umbrella forms), spread open at the top and divided into four segments, formed the market's ceiling such that they resembled the old market tents or *mantas*. These umbrellas were made of four hypar shells, which tapered to a central support or footing, inside which a pipe allowed rainwater to drain into the local sewerage system. Originally, the complex was painted only in black and white: the columns were black; the undersides of the umbrellas in the market's interior were white; and the structure's half-enclosing walls were covered with black mosaic tiles.

The shape of the interior space was not least of all determined by the required on-location lighting, which was to facilitate all market-related activities. So the light for the market was intense and rather bright. But a less harsh and more evenly distributed light was used for the individual stalls. Since the walls only framed the space and had no load-bearing function, the ordered arrangement of hypars made it possible to insert continuous ribbon windows between the rows of umbrellas and wall enclosure. Divided into 10 x 10-foot cubicles for the stalls, the umbrella-covered surface measures 35,000 square feet. From the floor to vaulting, the height of the interior measures 20 feet. Today the market still stands in Coyoacán, underneath the same sea of hypars. However, because the artistic value of the structure's exterior went unrecognized by some, it has been mutilated by a series of unsuccessful interventions.

Opposite page:
Mosaic-bearing medium-height partition walls comprise the sellers' stalls.

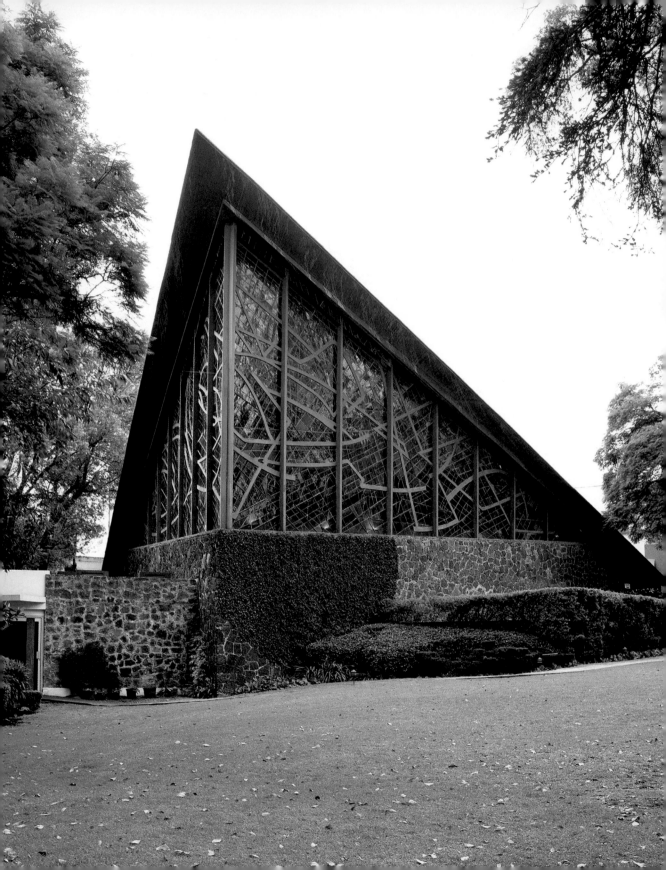

1955 ▸ Our Lady of Solitude Chapel, *El Altillo*

Coyoacán, Mexico City
Collaborating Architects: Enrique de la Mora and Fernando López Carmona

Opposite page:
The dramatic glazed tip of the church facing north

Right:
Staircase without railing leading to the crypt's chapel

Plan of the entire complex

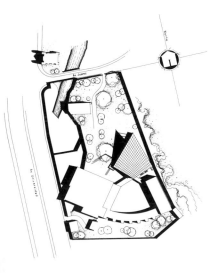

Coyoacán was the first village founded by conquistador Hernán Cortéz in the Anáhuac province. Relatively cut off from Mexico City until the beginning of the twentieth century, this region was known for its lush gardens and expansive estates, but it also epitomized the simple country life. Located in a dense garden with courtyard alongside a river, a colonial structure dating back to the eighteenth-century period of the viceroys was taken over by a religious order—the Missionaries of the Holy Spirit. In the middle of the twentieth century, when the congregation found it necessary to build a chapel as a center for the religious activities of its local parishioners here, the architects Enrique de la Mora and Fernando López Carmona (who regularly collaborated with Mora) were hired for the job. Together with Candela, they formed a work group for the design and the construction of a chapel dedicated to the Holy Virgin and still known today as *El Altillo*.

Since the parishioners of the diocese would not require a particularly large building, the project was mostly concerned with developing a moderately sized yet comfortable chapel that could serve as a meditation room for the order's missionaries as well. In view of the expansion of the property, which had to be transformed into a garden, a specific architectural problem had to be solved: how to design a building resigned not to lose itself in the garden without resorting to monumentality and making the project uneconomical. The solution was to a design a rhombus-shaped building with a north-to-south principal axis: a structure roofed over by an elegant doubly-curved roof shell, bordered by straight generators and relying on supports at its transverse axis. Since the thrust of both cantilevers are unequal, the shorter arm is

Church seen from the west

attached to concrete walls while the vertical cross at the entrance functions purely via tension. At the south side of the building, an entrance leads to the front of an inner courtyard (reinterpreted atrium) enclosed by three towering walls, which bear reliefs depicting the Stations of the Cross. The abstract design of a colored-glass wall by Kitzia Hofmann spreads out behind the altar at the north side of the sacred building, and Herbert Hofmann's metal sculpture of the Virgin Mary, to whom the chapel is dedicated, hangs enthroned at the crown of this expansive glazing. The interior furnishings (benches, prayer stools, kneelers, graphic elements) as well as the simple building materials (clay, undressed stone, mortar) are forerunners of the *etapa luminosa* of ecclesiastical building, which notably revived the three-dimensional design of Catholic churches in Mexico in the 1960s.

Remarkable about this solution is the fact that the differentiation of space in the building is achieved with one and the same physical element, based as it were on no more than differently elevated levels and nuances of light on the underside of the roof shell. The asymmetrically positioned rhombus made it possible to conceive a gallery for the public, accessible from an outside staircase above the entrance, whose floor projects out over the entrance below. Inside the church, visitors are immediately aware of the parabolic curve of the roof anchored to lateral cantilevers in the transverse axis.

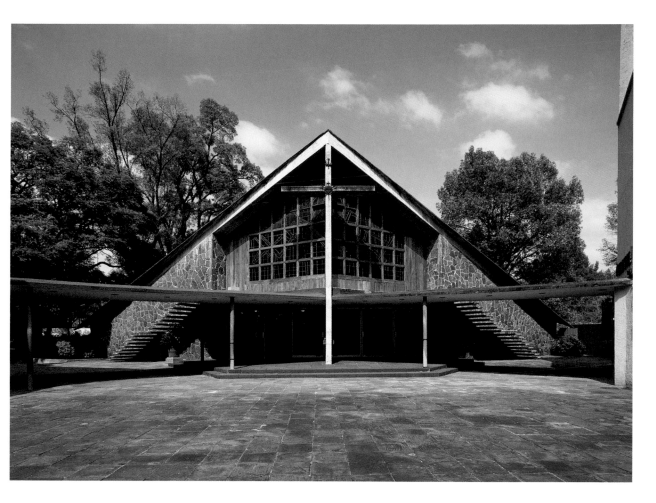

Church viewed from the south

Church interior before the glazing behind the altar was installed

41

The colored glazing designed by Kitzia Hofmann and the metal sculpture of the Virgin Mary by Herbert Hofmann

Only on closer inspection, however, does the roof's soaring underside reveal a wealth of scars—traces of the formwork used to form the concrete. Stretched out before visitors' eyes, the colored-glass wall seems to dissolve the interior's spatial boundaries. Here, too, pale-yellow hues—an almost Nordic luminance painted on the panes of glass—produce a shimmering and disconcerting effect, which seems to permeate the entire structure and its furnishings. This light reaches the aisles of the church and causes the hypar's edges to disappear. In turn, the interior space seems to push outward towards the building's exterior appearing to transcend the original limitations set by the architect. Outside the church, the viewer is aware of the rhomboid roof shell coming to rest on the stone base, but also of the vertical concrete crucifix from which the concrete shell would seem to hang.

Indirect light heightens the surface texture of the shells

Below:
Cross-section and plan

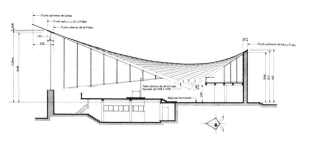

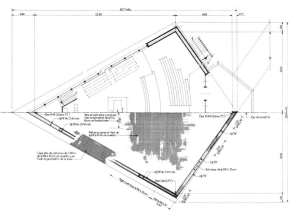

1955 ‣ Main Hall of Mexico's New Stock Exchange

Mexico City

Collaborating Architects: Enrique de la Mora and Fernando López Carmona

Interior

Colin Faber emphasizes how productive the joint efforts of Candela, de la Mora, and López Carmona were, and how often they resulted in reserved and tasteful works of architecture. This particular structure was the first cross vault ever designed in Candela's studio. The shell was developed from the fusion of two hypars on a 50 x 85-foot surface area at a height of approx. 30 feet from the floor to the crown of the arches. It stands on the third-floor extension of an existing eight-story office building (Mexico's Stock Exchange). Candela needed an entire year to solve all the problems connected with the curve-edged sections and set up four points of support for the umbrella-like structures, which turn into hypars in their ascent, merging in the overhead space like two rounded-arch barrel vaults in a Romanesque dome, except that in this case, because of the load distribution on the four corner points, the vaulting has to remain free of pressure and stress points. Referring to the progression of his research into concrete membranes, Candela later said: "[...] it was with the Stock Exchange Hall, working together with de la Mora and López Carmona, that I discovered how to really work with hypars. It was with this building that I began to study them."

Cross-section

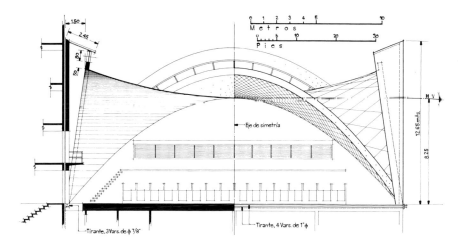

Opposite page:
Main Counter in the Stock Exchange Hall

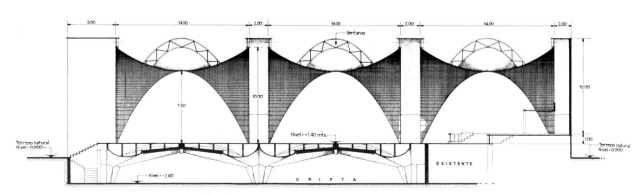

A - A

1956 ▸ Church of Saint Anthony of the Orchards

Mexico City

Collaborating Architects: Enrique de la Mora and Fernando López Carmona

Interior, looking towards the entrance

Opposite page, top:
Interior, looking towards the altar

Cross-section

While some of Candela's projects became artistic milestones on account of their aesthetic qualities alone, others present themselves as fundamentally important works because they bear witness to specific insights in the ever-evolving architectural thinking of their creator. This church belongs to the latter category. It stands on the edge of the old road to Mexico-Tlacopán, which formerly connected Tenochtitlan, the capital of the Old Mexican Empire, with the City of Tacuba. Although the church was never completed, Candela's design solution saw to it that the roofed-over interior space of the church was usable. Catholic religious services have been held here since 1956.

The task was to construct a church whose nave was spacious enough to accommodate the entire congregation. By the time Candela got involved in the project, a vault had been built under the presbytery and its inflexible concrete frame was intended to serve as the load-bearer for a structure with "traditional" qualities—meaning with

Multicolored strips of glazing join at the base point.

The exterior divulges none of the interior's spatial complexity.

concrete arches resting on walls and columns. From the floor to the ceiling, the vault offered a useful 9-foot-tall volume under the floor, a space that addressed the clients' desire to have a crypt installed here. The chosen solution required constructing two star-shaped reticulated vaults, each one formed by twelve hypar segments and positioned on four corner posts. The entire complex bridged the width of the church while supporting both the floor and the net load of the church space directly above it. The new reticulated vaults measured 52 x 52 feet, and the structure installed above the hypars made it possible to pass over the uneven umbrella shells to the level floor area of the church.

In the case of this structure, Candela's innovation involved using the knowledge acquired with the vault for the Stock Exchange Hall. This time, however, he incorporated a complex of three cross vaults (the Stock Exchange Hall used only one) formed from free-edged hypars, and therefore without ridges. This covered an area of 53 x 155 feet while sustaining a minimum height of 25 feet and a constant thickness of 4 cm. The structural loads were deflected to twelve corner points, with the cross vaults

themselves transferring the load to the foundations. Here Candela did more than reduce the thickness of the concrete membrane. Simultaneously, he eliminated unnecessary elements by proving that the incurring stress exactly followed the lines formed by the unfolding and fusing of the paraboloids. Light enters the space through glazed strips between arches and the lateral curves of the façades, which border the space and bear only their own weight.

Photographs taken during the construction clearly reveal the beauty of the formwork: the vertically and horizontally positioned boards shown together with the necessary diagonals required to keep the scaffolding from collapsing on the one hand, and the hundreds of approx. 2-inch-wide wooden boards following the guiding lines for the production of paraboloids on the other. All this makes visible the complex, bold movements of the geometric surfaces in space.

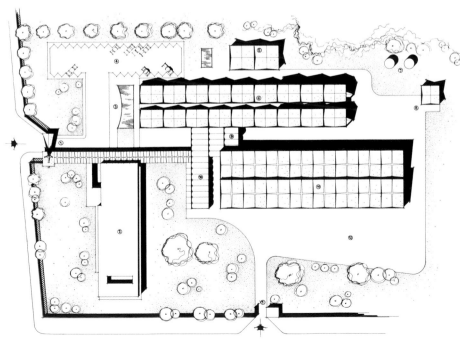

1956 ‣ Factory Gate of the Lederle Laboratories

Mexico City

Collaborating Architect: Alejandro Prieto

Opposite page, top:
Entrance, 1956

Opposite page, bottom:
Plan of entire complex

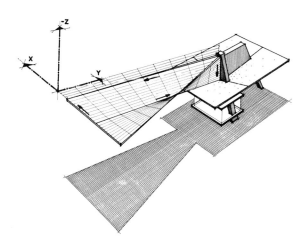

Perspective view

In the early 1950s, when pharmaceutical laboratories began to be built on the periphery of Mexico City, federally funded aid programs encouraged the establishment of production centers of foreign pharmaceutical firms. Candela's geometry-based formal language expressed through members made of reinforced concrete found a further application in these industrial structures: it proved ideal for conceiving the kind of multifunctional, large-scale, and brightly lit factory spaces required by industrial production. Later, however, the same industrialization that made these spaces possible led to the demolition or remodeling of many of the buildings Candela constructed for this type of complex. The reason for tearing them down was because the land on which they stood had increased in value and was put to different uses now that it had become part of the city center, for the same plot of land located on the periphery of Mexico City in the 1950s belonged to the capital's inner city by the beginning of the twentieth century.

Among the aforementioned industrial enterprises to set up branches here was Lederle, whose architectural design is credited to Alejandro Prieto. Every possible type of geometric variation appeared on its 963,000 square feet of built-up property: umbrellas, domes, butterflies, vaults, and cones. Especially rich in variety was the design of the control booth area at the factory gate: higher than the medium-height surrounding factory walls, a glazed booth was positioned between two almost overlapping umbrella constructions of different heights. While the lower roof connects with a covered passageway leading to the production building, the upper roof stands parallel to the road, assuming a monumental position in midair, its wing jutting out over the street, where vehicles pass under it like a bridge. The folded slab is anchored to the ground on a concrete tripod. Like the majority of Candela's structures, the 43-foot-long concrete roof executes a twist in midair as it projects forward. It consists of two sloped slabs. Attached to the tripod on a vertical plane, these gradually turn, unfold, and transform into a hyperbolic paraboloid, and ultimately produce a double hypar in the form of a fan.

1957 ‣ Jamaica Wholesale Market

Mexico City

Architectural Design: Municipal Urban Planning Department

Opposite page:
View of the loading docks

Snapshots taken of the market

In the early 1950s, the city council of Mexico City initiated a program for the restoration of its markets. This included planning a central wholesale market to be built on a 588,500 square-foot area. Since the time of the viceroys, shipments of vegetables, lettuce, flowers and fruit arrived in Mexico City via "Jamaica," a district in the southeast of the city bordering the old historical center. The municipal authorities in charge of the project chose to continue the tradition of the market and simply rebuild the facilities here. Candela's membranes of tested concrete offered an ideal solution for the architectural task: to construct roof surfaces whose umbrella shells would offer ample space for market stands as well as protection from rain and prolonged exposure to sunlight. Since trucks delivering fresh produce (140 vehicles per ramp) required their own loading and unloading docks, the task would also entail designing such areas for customers and sellers alike.

Candela chose to work with two parallel rows of twelve umbrella shells, each measuring 60 x 60 feet. To avoid any bending at the edges of the umbrella forms, the hypars' curves were slightly strengthened by dividing each member into eight sections. This was one of the clearest demonstrations of Candela's architectural thinking at work: he solved the problem by altering the form and not by increasing the material's density or working with edge beams, tie members, or any other additional element. Still, the market ensemble made a somewhat contradictory and perhaps unusual impression because it ran contrary to the customary ways in which people view things: it featured a huge roof shell whose umbrellas endowed it with openness and a sense of movement; yet, despite the missing walls, its single roof seemed to offer all the solid and encompassing protection of a building. If ever there was a moment when twentieth-century architectural thinking was freed from the standard four-walls concept, then this—in the form of Candela's shells—was it.

Cross-section

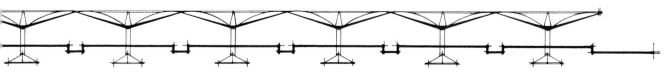

1957 ▸ *La Jacaranda* Nightclub

Acapulco, Guerrero
Collaborating Architect: Juan Sordo Madaleno

La Jacaranda seen from the sea

Opposite page:
The hypar during construction

Below:
Site plan

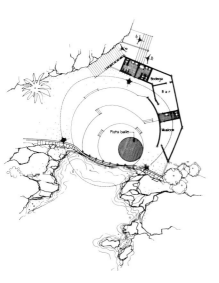

In the middle of the 1950s, the *El Presidente* hotel, a typical rectangular tower in the International Style, was erected on Acapulco Bay—Mexico's world-famous tourist harbor in an elegant coastal district, an area that underwent considerable development after 1950. The architect Juan Sordo Madaleno, whose complete works are characterized by an elegance of proportions and a minute attention to detail, was responsible for the design of this hotel built on the same level as the coastal road skirting the bay. Just a few yards below the hotel, with a view of the sea, Candela erected the now demolished, concrete shell of the *La Jacaranda* nightclub.

Among Candela's many creations there are two buildings whose uniqueness owes much to the successful fusing of their forms with bodies of water: *Los Manantiales* restaurant in Xochimilco and *La Jacaranda* nightclub in Acapulco. The nightclub stood close to the beach on a terrace, separated from the sea by only a strip of sand covered with palms and rock formations. To see it from the beach while walking toward the sea was to see a structure resembling a wind-filled *manta* or tent-like structure. It was as though a powerful gust of wind had toppled a dome on three supports. Viewed from the hotel, the shell resembled an enormous swelling sail or oversized seashell, and both impressions harmonized with the natural setting of the beach. The decision to install the nightclub under the laterally open membrane shell—giving the impression that a breeze kept it "inflated"—created the desired contrast to the hotel's functional structure.

The structure of the nightclub was developed from the fusion of three hypars on three support points, covering an almost triangular site whose surface area measured 3,200 square feet. The restaurant and dance floor were distributed over three levels. The sanitary facilities and bar were located in an adjacent extension separate from the vault. The paraboloid jutted so far out that not even rays of sunlight at a 45-degree angle could enter the nightclub. As a result, the interior was constantly protected from direct sunlight. The way in which nature is drawn into the architecture, using the simplest of means, makes *La Jacaranda* in Acapulco a key structure indeed.

In his essay *En defensa del formalismo* ("In Defense of Formalism"), perhaps written while this work was in progress, Candela insisted on the importance of intuition, which he considered the ideal way to approach the design of form. Although he constantly spoke in favor of mathematical and statistical calculations for determining the configuration of structures, these were hardly what he considered the best means with which to define a structure's features. Current tendencies, criticized Candela, went so far as to claim "[...] that structural analysis can provide the form of a structure [...]."

1957 ▸ Entranceway Sculpture at *Lomas Tropicales de Tequesquitengo*

Tequesquitengo, Morelos
Collaborating Architects: Guillermo Rosell and Manuel Larrosa

Candela's sculpture indicates the entrance to the *Lomas Tropicales de Tequesquitengo* housing colony.

The Tequesquitengo is a lake in the state of Morelos, a state bordering Mexico City. From the 1940s onward, Morelos was a recreation area for tourists and local inhabitants. In the 1950s, however, when widespread municipal development and the construction of vacation housing began, the real estate along Lake Tequesquitengo was systematically urbanized. Beginning in 1957 the housing colony *Lomas Tropicales de Tequesquitengo* was occupied, and it was important for the colony's developers that the complex had a physical landmark that accentuated the new colony's situation in the landscape, not least of all because of the region's lack of manmade features at the time.

Candela was commissioned to design a geometric work that functioned as both a "municipal sculpture" and a marker indicating the entrance to the grounds of the housing colony. Since its function was merely ornamental, he chose to use the horizon as background, with the sculpture's large scale as a visual eye-catcher. Candela's sculpture seems inspired by a seesaw. Two concrete slabs secured at opposite ends of a framework continually rise and fall, their movements perfectly balanced by the static weight of tension rods. In the design of this structure occupying 50 x 105 feet and a maximum height of 25 feet, two fan-like concrete forms face one another. Their lower sections are joined by four suspension rods and four tension rods. Each fan consists

56

of two triangular hypars joined to form a four-faceted triangle from whose tip the lower strut extends. Above these, tension rods absorb the resulting stress from the weight of the outspread fans. Viewed in its entirety, the entranceway sculpture is a quasi large-scale *divertimento*, pushing the powers of resistance displayed by Candela's applied geometry to their limits.

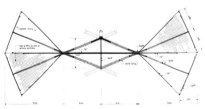

Plan

Top:
Sidelong view

1958 ▸ Plaza of the Fans (Plaza *Los Abanicos*)

Lomas de Cuernavaca, Morelos
Collaborating Architects: Guillermo Rosell and Manuel Larrosa

Opposite page:
The sculpture stands in a pool of water laid out in elevations along a sloped street.

Sculpture seen from the street

Plan of the entire complex

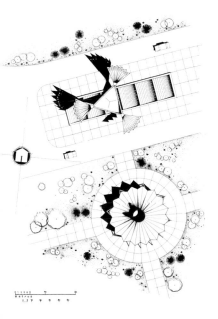

In the middle of the 1950s, in the south of Cuernavaca—a city located in the state of Morelos, and whose favorable climate made it a popular spot for Mexico City inhabitants to spend their summer vacation—an expansive land development for creating a new residential district was launched. Symbolic of this initiative, a municipal symbol raises itself up on the Plaza of the Fans (Plaza *Los Abanicos*): an open-air sculpture, with tube-like elements for emitting playful jets of water, erected over a large-scale fountain. Encountered in Cuernavaca's semitropical environment, visitors see the sculpture as a sign of welcome. But not least of all for the sculpture, even today people enjoy driving out to the housing colony, which was called Lomas de Cuernavaca when it was founded.

Architecturally, the goal was to build a structure whose cleverly geometric formal language would both animate and accentuate the entrance to the residential district. On a triangular base, intersecting edge beams shoot upward on three sides. Their lower sections embrace three hypars, and their upper sections the bundle of fan-like folded surfaces that give the sculpture its name. The three fan-like surfaces remain balanced thanks to the help of the horizontal tie rods holding them together. A noticeable contrast exists between the edge beams and the folded surfaces: the beams are thick, the surfaces are thin. Each fan has ten folds perforated with small holes. At first glance, the edge beams seem ill-proportioned compared to the paraboloids' dimensions. But their design is, after all, based on their importance as counterparts to the upper folded sections, and they have the important function of fortifying the sculpture's lower section as well. Like most of Candela's structures, at

Commercial center beside the sculpture

the time of its completion the sculpture kept its natural concrete colors. Today, however, the sculpture's exterior is painted white and its interior sections painted blue. Seen alongside another work by Candela, a pavilion built on the same grounds, the sculpture gently accentuates the landscape. Although, according to Candela himself, the zigzag form seems "perhaps a bit surreal," Bruno Zevi spoke of "plastic structuralism" here.

In his study of Candela's complete works, Buschiazzo pays special attention to structure. He points out that the works made of concrete can be understood only if their structure is regarded as a leitmotif: "[Candela] protests [in his writings] against the way reinforced concrete is commonly used nowadays, namely in an anachronistic and atavistic manner, which imitates specific structural solutions meant especially for iron and wood, and whose practice fatally leads to prismatic works." Returning to Candela's essay *Divagaciones estructurales en torno al estilo* again, we read: "Reinforced concrete is not meant to be used in blocks of mass or, put more clearly, in rectangular blocks, even though this is how we see it used today. As forms, rectangular columns made of tested concrete are as absurd and archaic as door lintels, and they obey the same phenomenon of constructive mimesis." Considering the rotation of its forms and the entire construction's stability, which adds no more than form itself as an

element, *Los Abanicos* clearly proves the accuracy of these thoughts on a suitable type of construction.

Facing *Los Abanicos*, on the same property, Candela constructed a circular structure whose roof shell is shaped like a fully opened fan. An outer tension ring absorbs the thrusts of 32 concrete segments, all of them hypars, which rest on sloped supports and form triangles. The entire system is balanced by an inner roof-ring subjected to pressure at the structure's center. Originally intended as a shop for the residential area, today the interior of this remodeled building serves different purposes. Compared to Candela's other works, however, what seems missing here is a solution displaying a better sense of proportions. Although the roof shell obviously presents itself in the form of a delicate element engaged in virtual movement, the decision to use supports in the form of triangles was hardly the most successful of formal solutions.

1958 ▸ *Los Manantiales* Restaurant
Xochimilco, Mexico City
Collaborating Architects: Fernando and Joaquín Álvarez Ordóñez

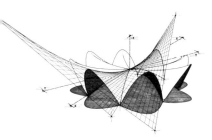

Above:
Schematic drawing of flowerlike shell construction composed of hypar sections

Xochimilco is a township of pre-Hispanic origin in the south of Mexico City. Up to the beginning of the twentieth century it was the principal supplier of the capital's drinking water. The original springs over time formed a lake which was used by the indigenous inhabitants to water their crops. At that time, the locals cultivated their land by producing artificial islands made of mud from the bed of the lake, but also from sections of earth-covered wood-and-reed rafting. This type of root system known as a *chinampa*, in effect a raft anchored in the lake, was planted over with flowers and vegetables. This explains the township's name, Xochimilco, which derives from the

Right:
Rooftop view

Nahuátl dialect and means "place where the flowers grow." Throughout the twentieth century, Xochimilco was a recreation area for the inhabitants of Mexico City, who came here every Sunday to row a *trajinera* (typical Xochimilco-style wooden boat), stroll along the lake, admire the "floating gardens," and relax in the beauty of what was so rare for Mexico—a landscape inundated with canals. Here, on a small lakeside peninsula surrounded by *chinampas*, Candela constructed a restaurant among the most beautiful structures in the annals of twentieth-century architecture. It owes its name, *Los Manantiales*, to its natural environment: *manantial* means "source" or "fountain."

The architectural task was to build an establishment whose 1,000-person seating capacity would replace the previous wooden-structured restaurant destroyed by fire. Candela and his partners decided to build an octagonal groined vault composed of four intersecting hypars. Inside the building, eight groins marking the surface sections

Opposite page:
This overall view shows the melding of exterior and interior space.

Los Manantiales viewed from the water

converge at the center of the structure. The result is a lotus shape on a surface area approx. 140 feet in diameter, overshadowed by hypars measuring 85 x 100 feet at their points of support on the floor, and with an overall height of 28 feet. At the restaurant's center, however, the height reduces to 20 feet. Later, Candela often recalled that his solutions for this project were so successful because they were directly linked with choosing the correct means to convert the geometric shape into physical reality and translate it to a concrete membrane, but also with the carefully handled details, which linked the structure to the earth. During this project, his fully matured technological intuition told him not to use edge beams (the shell functioned without edge stress) and to concentrate on deflecting the loads to the supports instead. This resulted in the edge stress being transferred to the groins, but also in the vertical loads being absorbed by the point-like footing at the base of the structure. A ring-shaped tension

Interior

member absorbed the lateral thrust of the shells. Here the beholder is overwhelmed by the calming, radial gestures of concrete waves, which seem to hover just above the earth's surface without touching it. While the effect devised for *La Jacaranda* quickly exhausted in Acapulco, insofar as the viewer imagines a sea breeze unevenly filling a soft membrane, in the case of *Los Manantiales*, with the sea breeze missing, the viewer senses lines generated by waves whose grace and simplicity repeat the sea's undulations in the third dimension. This creates a lotus blossom in the floating garden of Xochimilco.

The glazed façades of the parabolic surfaces (formed by the hypars' design) offer protection from the weather while producing a weightless architecture dominated by glass.

1959 ▸ Lomas de Cuernavaca Chapel

Lomas de Cuernavaca, Morelos

Collaborating Architects: Guillermo Rosell and Manuel Larrosa

Opposite page:
Overall view

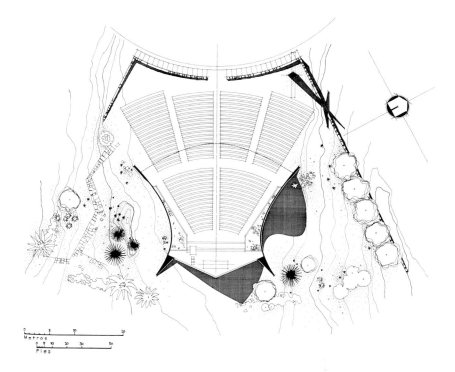

Site plan

Lomas de Cuernavaca Chapel is a mark on the horizon, a swiftly shaped curve that seems drawn on the sky with a piece of graphite. If ever Candela explored the limits of abstraction, it had to be during the period when he completed the design of this small structure (hardly larger than 100 x 100 feet), which functions like a membrane filled with the air of a sudden breeze.

Located on the ridge of a hill in the same valley where the Plaza of the Fans lies, the chapel is more of an architectural than a religious symbol of a municipal structure dedicated to the renewal of social objectives. Although intended for religious services of the Catholic faith, it displays no elements of that tradition. The architects responsible for the chapel's design exhausted the small budget at their disposal. They designed a triangular platform with raked rows of pews for worshippers; a concrete cross whose arms evolve from triangular facets; and a roof shell with a heavily shaded gullet or throat section, which offers fresh air to the congregation—a curved hypar whose largest parabola is 75 feet high and measures 100 feet at its base. When the chapel was constructed, before the presence of trees and other buildings distracted from the clarity of its architectural concept, the structure was sharply silhouetted against the sky.

Candela's use of free-edged hypars pushed the chapel's geometric construction to the limits of its stability-producing possibilities. According to Colin Faber, Candela saw his experimental free-edge procedure as the ultimate refinement of a particular phase of building research. Yet this hardly meant that the thin shell had exhausted all its possibilities.

Although the chapel's shell is formed by a single paraboloid, Candela suggests a pair of hypars by brilliantly playing with the two drastically differing heights of the arches developed from the diagonal curves. The parabola-shaped arch behind the altar rises to a height of 28 feet and features a glass window that not only admits light that

The building viewed from the side

Detail of the altar

Church interior seen from the entrance side

Schematic drawing of the shell model

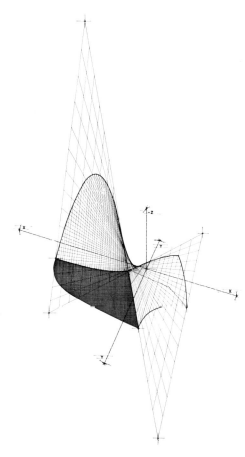

delicately illuminates the sacred area, but also offers a commanding view of the landscape and bordering mountains of the Cuernavaca Valley. The ends of the smallest arch of the transverse paraboloid, which rises no higher than 14 feet, anchor the entire structure to the ground.

Viewers are immediately taken by this architectural space. Even the traces of the formwork, visible on the downward-curving concrete surfaces, help convey a sense of newly established dynamics, and further emphasize a visitor's submersion into the depths of the building. In turn, the distinction between top and bottom, as well as between landscape and interior space, dissolves. Due to the roof shell's design, the area in front of the altar is plunged in shadow, producing an indescribable spatial phenomenon: the shadow's inversion, caused by the undulating wave of the shell.

1959 ▸ Church of Saint Joseph the Laborer

Monterrey, Nuevo León
Collaborating Architects: Enrique de la Mora and Fernando López Carmona

Entrance

Opposite page:
Interior

In this church, erected on the outskirts of Monterrey, one of northeastern Mexico's major cities, Candela returned to the technique of aligning geometric figures without actually having them merge. He used the same method to build the Church of Our Miraculous Lady, where the hypars on every side of the church nave function independently, and the space of the nave develops through the hypars' frontal approximation. With the Church of Saint Joseph the Laborer, two gigantic hypars with straight and asymmetrical edges face one another on a 85 x 100-foot surface area. The sections' inner surfaces—upward-curving hyper paraboloids almost forming 90-degree angles—are connected by tension rods 2.5 cm in diameter. The edge beams extend exactly from the baseline of the wings and down to imposts on the ground.

What makes the structure so remarkable is the clear relationship between the stress and the equalization of pressure and tension. Viewed frontally, each hypar is held upright thanks to the existence of the other, but also connected to it by tensile force. Slender ties allow for a generous, colored glazing between and along the edges of the wings. The entrance and altar, which face one another, lie under the vertical alignment of the two hypars.

This type of three-dimensional, structural solution created a building whose profile altogether differed from those of Candela's previous structures. Admittedly, both hypars (measuring from tip to tip 180 feet) effortlessly rise up higher than the ribbon windows and convey a sense of weightlessness by hovering above the ground. Nevertheless, the allocation of functions in the interior space lacks the same degree of perfection found in other structures by Candela. Here the real topic of discussion is perhaps the changing of symbolic values expressed through the handling of the light. In the case of *El Altillo* chapel, for example, the structural details with regard to light are extremely clear: the greatest amount of light focuses on the altar, which increases the dramatic effect in the presbytery. In Saint Joseph the Laborer, the altar stands in darkness while light concentrates on the sides of the church nave. In his study of the building, Buschiazzo questions this in particular: "Is it legitimate or logical to use forms or lighting to accentuate central zones not connected with the altar, the most important point in the church for the staging of services? Is there really an agreement between the concept and the function here?" Not only does the area reserved for the altar receive far too little attention, the entrance, too, seems somewhat overlooked and gloomy, positioned at the very lowest point where the hypars meet.

Section drawing

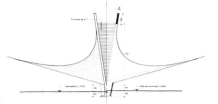

1959–1960 ▸ San Vicente de Paul Chapel

Coyoacán, Mexico City

Collaborating Architects: Enrique de la Mora and Fernando López Carmona

Opposite page:
Interior

The headpieces worn by the nuns of the order inspired the design of the church roof.

Shell model and section drawing

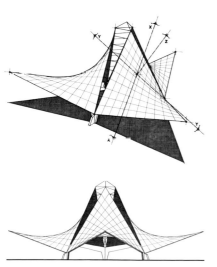

In 1955 Candela built *El Altillo* together with Enrique de la Mora and Fernando López Carmona. Only five years later, a different congregation—the Sisters of San Vicente de Paul (Hermanas paulistas)—commissioned the same architects to construct their chapel as well. In the collective consciousness of Mexico City's inhabitants, Coyoacán is thought of as a city on the outskirts with dense green areas and woods, and it was on a piece of property fitting this description that the "Hermanas" erected a senior citizens' home for which the chapel was very important.

In contrast to other projects, the available plot of land was rather limited here. The site-specific task involved was how to develop, between the senior citizens' home and the chapel, a route that would spare the residents both a long walk and over-exertion.

The chosen solution uses equally surprising floor and elevation plans. These develop from a surface area composed of isosceles triangles, whose bases produce another triangle (this time with equilateral sides) in which the presbytery is located. The roof shell consists of three straight-edged hypars yielding approx. 4,800 square feet of interior space whose principal axis measures 66 feet, with a shorter axis measuring 50 feet. Each hypar has an average thickness of 4 cm and is secured to the ground on two imposts. The triangular supports are given small perpendicular wings that function as abutments. Like in *El Altillo*, the hypars are asymmetrical, because a portion of the shell curves upward. The vertical element coincides with the area of the altar, which forms the harmonious center of the entire complex. Vertically elevated concrete shells compensate for the cantilever of the front section. All three upward-

oriented shells or enclosures are connected by steel rods, which absorb the tensile
force. Colin Faber calls the design solution for the latticework structure between the
shells that balances the three hypars "pure Candela," because it is a harmonizing
compromise between the building's structure and aesthetics, achieved here by three
strips of colored glass.

As usual with Candela's structural solutions, the mechanics of the shells are
detectable with the naked eye: without facing or any visual deceptions, the loads of
what appear to be falling membranes are stabilized by the vertical "stitched areas."
Ultimately, the solution displays a double virtuosity: on a purely three-dimensional
level, the roof's form suggests the special headpiece worn by nuns and made of three
folded bands of fabric, while the architectural objective is met by giving priority to the
north-south axis, beginning at the north entrance—below the choir loft—and ending at
the altar. With its rows of pews for the congregation, the church nave harmonizes with

Altar

every hypar. Light is admitted into the space through ventilation louvers that afford a view of the garden at the same time. On entering the chapel from a hallway in the senior citizens' home (after passing through a modest doorway measuring no more than 5 x 7 feet), the richness of the chapel's space instantly overwhelms. While the chapel project was underway, Candela mastered the subject of structural stability, and, for their part, the collaborating architects knew exactly how to make liturgical space harmonize with Candela's structural views.

1960 ▸ Bacardi & Co. Bottling Plant

Cuautitlán, State of Mexico
Collaborating Architects: Saenz-Cancio-Martín-Álvarez and Gutiérrez
Engineering Consultant: Luis Torres Landa

Photograph taken during construction
Only three cross vaults were produced during the first building phase.

Toward the end of the 1950s, Bacardi & Co. commissioned Candela to design and construct its factory buildings intended for use as a bottling plant and warehouses. This would be a thoroughly modern complex whose architectural quality was expected to attract (financial) recognition. While Candela designed the company's production halls, Mies van der Rohe designed its office buildings.

Candela's solution called for six free-edged cross vaults, with lateral lengths of 100 feet, constructed on a quadrilateral ground plan. Each vault derives from the fusion of two hypars whose deepest points, located in the corners of the ground plan's square, end at supports that continue the sloped line of the paraboloid to the ground. Candela took full advantage of the paraboloid's natural slant to insert transparent ribbon windows between every two vaults, and, together with glazed surfaces along the horizontal boundaries of the space, these contributed to the bright lighting required by industrial work. The 100-foot area is perfectly justified. It represents the most reasonable limit for supporting the approx. 4 cm-thick membranes at the crown of a portable framework, but at the same time ensures the typical delicacy of the concrete shells.

Opposite page:
Present-day state of the wall glazing reaching to the ground

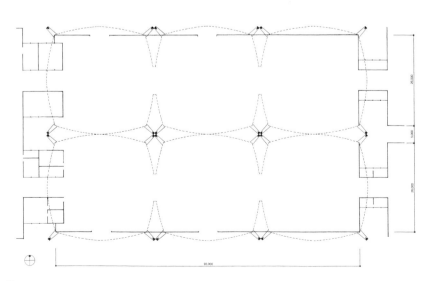

Above:
Interior view of the first building phase

Left:
Candela designed the factory's cafeteria as well.

Opposite page, top and bottom left:
Bottling plant interior

Opposite page, bottom right:
Ground-floor plan

1960 ‣ Santa Monica Church

Mexico City

Collaborating Architect: Fernando López Carmona

Opposite page:
Interior, whose sloped columns absorb the load of the supported shells

The majority of the buildings Candela constructed were completed on expansive sites with commanding views of the surrounding countryside. Yet the Santa Monica Church was built on an L-shaped piece of urban property with two fronts, one of which faces a park surrounding a small chapel of colonial origin. Building on this property was difficult, and the main architectural objective was to position the building in such a way that would allow it to accommodate the estimated number of worshippers. At the same time, however, the question remained as to what design was appropriate for the sacred structure, which stood out in this residential area because of its size alone.

The solution amounted to establishing a semicircular ground plan at the corner of the site, and positioning at its crown a sloped support around which the roof-forming hypar segments came together. Paradoxically, the hypars seemed to emanate from a vertical strut—an impression caused by the assumed function of the interrelated forms, which have no connection at all with the supporting strut's geometry. Compared to Candela's other buildings, the façade of the church displays a higher degree of complexity, especially when compared with the large-scale dimensions of the Barcardi Bottling Plant and the proportions of the Cuernavaca Chapel. In the Santa Monica Church, the hypars are arranged in pairs and develop into fan-like forms. But following the generators of the upper edges, the gaps between the hypars are used to install glazed insets, which admit afternoon light into the church. The slope of each hypar is interrupted by a triangle used to deflect the structure's loads to the ground. These triangular surfaces received glazing, as did the church doors.

The appearance of this church is defined by two elements: the typical construction of sacred Catholic buildings with their large capacity, and the density of urban-planning developments. Embedded in a modern residential district, the Santa Monica Church came into being as a new social symbol that would stand out by virtue of the dimensions of its architecture.

Below:
Exterior

1966 ▸ La Florida Church
Naucalpan, State of Mexico

Opposite page:
Exterior
Originally the roof was a light concrete-gray color with yellow-toned brick for the wall surfacing. The autonomy of the roof shell was greatly altered by the coat of red paint applied later.

Interior

Above:
The lantern viewed from below

By the early 1960s it was evident that two qualities characterized the work completed under Candela's leadership: originality, which invigorated his architectural thinking, and low construction costs. In conjunction with a large-scale land development in the north of Mexico City, the new parish of La Florida Housing Colony earned Candela a contract for the construction of their Catholic mission. The site offered the possibility of developing a circular ground plan, and this allowed the building to appear rhythmic without favoring a particular direction. The concrete shell best suited to the circular plan was a cross vault composed of eight hypars. Compared to similar solutions by Candela, here the building's main distinguishing feature was a small lantern-like form attached to a second level, which, while repeating the model of eight upward-bending structural segments (leaves), produced another cross vault. This crowning element was mounted to a compressed ring, and its polychromatic panes contribute to the coloring of the space.

Once again a successfully resolved detail contributed to the aesthetic completion of an entire building. But even the first conceptual plans for the church called for the aesthetic additive of a concrete shell's virtual "wing," which not only offered shade, but also defined the opening that allowed light to enter—this being another of Candela's architectural paradoxes: that his rigid concrete shells were able to impart a sense of flight and weightlessness.

1967 ‣ San Lázaro Subway Station

Mexico City
**Architectural Design for the STC (Sistema de Transporte Colectivo) Subway
System: Julio Michel Sinner**

Exterior

Opposite page:
Interior

In 1967 Mexico City's municipal administration launched the operation of the No.1 line of the city's subway system (*Sistema de Transporte Colectivo*), marking the first time that public transportation facilities were built in Mexico City's difficult subsoil. This required extremely complicated engineering procedures, and Candela was asked to assist with the construction of three subway stations. Visually, the San Lázaro station was the most original of the three Candela constructed, but also the most original of all the stations on this subway line.

San Lázaro, an old quarter in the east of the city's historical center, had thrived on the edge of Tenochtitlán Island since the time of the Aztec empire. During the period of the viceroys and up to the beginning of the twentieth century, it was known as a trading center; later as a train station; and, since the end of the 1960s, as a subway transit junction. While this says something of the centuries-old infrastructure here, the difficulties with the subsoil cannot be overlooked. In Mexico City, a thick layer of extremely moist clay lies below the uppermost lining of the earth's crust. So the foundation soil for construction is perpetually muddy, not to mention the fact that the San Lázaro station complex lies in an area that was a lake until as late as the end of the nineteenth century.

Built on the corner of a plaza, the station building consists of two overlapping groups of hypars with straight-running edge beams. In its interior, the four supports of its cross-shaped ground plan taper downward to the foundations. Installed in the gaps between assorted hypars of varying heights are glazed light-admitting insets. The entrances are located at the corners of a square ground plan. Among the project's most fascinating achievements is its combination of double-height space with the dynamic spatial experience of encountering an indeterminate number of passageways, which, when viewing the structure from the plaza, gives rise to a thoroughly unexpected interior monumentality.

Inside the station, the sunlight, which enters at a low angle, contributes to the modeling of the space, whose wide range of interior hypars and traffic routes point to a new structural type in the urban landscape. It was not until the end of the 1960s that Mexico City became acquainted with mass-transport facilities and exhilarating speeds never experienced before. In Mexico, the interior design of San Lázaro station, with its wealth of connections, became the prototype of *no lugares* or non-place architecture, in which an actual site is characterized by incessant movement. In spite of this, the station's peculiar forms grant it an unmistakable identity, and this has left its mark on the city's collective memory. One of the station's most striking architectural qualities is the utter control of scale, from the tips of its hypars to its entrances. On entering the subway station, visitors are immediately astounded by the soaring lightness of the hyperbolic paraboloids.

1967 ▸ Candelaria Subway Station
Mexico City

Interior seen from the middle axis

Erected in the same district as the San Lázaro station, this station, too, is on the No.1 line. Candela was responsible for constructing the lobby of this subway station located in a quarter originally known as the *Candelaria* ("Duck Pond"). Linked to the same tradition as the San Lázaro Quarter, the Candelaria Quarter was formerly one of the old ports where shipments of vegetables, fruit, and plants from other regions arrived in the city.

Unlike the way that Candela had participated in other projects, here he was only the external planner and not the concrete-shell designer. Significant about this architecture is the fact that the foyer passes directly over the train platforms and runs parallel to the tracks. Candela erected two halls of hypars and connected them using a series of slender concrete struts. Strips of sash bars framing panes of glass hold the opposing membranes together. Light enters the space through this band as well as through the multicolored glazed windows on the lateral walls. Candela provided each hall with an axis composed of eleven umbrella columns, whose diameters assume a star shape. The leaves of the hypars extend from the top of each column, and, as these shapes resembling palm trees multiply, their fan-like crowns appear to blanket the space. The umbrellas measure 20 x 48 feet, which is repeated twenty-two times with eleven

Multicolored glazing on the upper level

symmetrical umbrella columns. Not including the continuous opening in the station's center, the umbrellas cover a width of about 93 feet.

The structural task posed the question of how best to attach the leaves of the hypars to each support. What finally developed was the image of a flexibly curving group of fans, which unfold to only a small degree and have no more than minimal contact with their counterparts. This produced a powerful light-and-dark effect never seen before in Candela's work. Although he frequently said that he never feared copying his own solutions, each new work tended to present a new detail that was often the result of an experiment based on the study of geometry or membrane-stress equations. In this case, we see for the first time the leaves or shells of hypars with a short span, but given a greatly extended depth. And these allowed their creator to utilize an entirely new light-and-dark effect. It should not be forgotten, however, that ever since designing the Cosmic Rays Pavilion, Candela often concentrated on aesthetic solutions that involved the use of light and shadow, and that twenty years later, with his inventiveness far from exhausted, he continued using these visual effects to produce novel solutions.

1968 ▸ Olympic Sports Complex
Mexico City
Collaborating Architects: Antoní Peyri and Enrique Castañeda Tamborrel

Built in scarcely eighteen months, this structure was designed for the 1968 Olympic Games in Mexico City. It could be considered "Candela's legacy" in Mexico, since three years later, in 1971, he emigrated to the United States and remained there until his death. What also makes the stadium a legacy is that, following its completion, Candela never again worked as an independent employer or structural engineer, but rather as a private consultant. But what makes it a legacy most is the quality of the structural solution, which Candela—as a builder with a sense of responsibility—achieved in conjunction with the specified ethical boundaries of his architecture. Several years prior to this project, he had established the fact that concrete membranes reached the limits of their economical capabilities and structural logic when shells measuring 100 feet in diameter were used, and that producing a larger shell was possible but not necessarily practical. For this reason, he decided against using the tested concrete for the sports complex. Instead, he used arched girders made of steel piping.

Here the problems to be solved were linked with the lack of time and the economical factors, but also with the enormous capacity involved, the resulting expansive dimensions, and the fulfilling of a political sense of purpose, insofar as the structure had to prove itself a permanent fixture. The 1968 Olympic Games in Mexico gave the country the chance to show the architectural world the extent to which it had matured twenty years after the construction of the University City, which quickly became a key work of modernism in Latin America. While a few existing buildings in the city were transformed into locations for sports events, other structures, such as the Olympic Stadium, were newly built for the occasion. Like many of Candela's architectural works, the stadium's monumentality and three-dimensional presence made it a milestone in the history of modernism. At the same time the stadium satisfied all the requirements listed in the project's brief: grandstands with a 20,000-spectator seating capacity, a playing court 266 feet in diameter, and a minimum height of 133 feet at the structure's center. Although a wide range of competition designs were submitted, the only one whose structural logic and material-related economy guaranteed the stadium's completion within the specified eighteen-month deadline was the proposal submitted by Candela and his partners. Years later, he recalled: "One night I just went home and sketched out the structure exactly the way it was built later, without any doubts in my mind about it [...]."

Within fifteen days all the questions relevant to the entire project's architecture had to be answered. The solution consisted of having two crossing rows of arches of different load-bearing distances develop the space of the flattened segment of a sphere. The curved lattice girders, averaging 17 feet in height, intersect every 46 feet and produce, in Candela's own words, "[...] surfaces never rectangular. In the center are

Opposite page:
Overall view

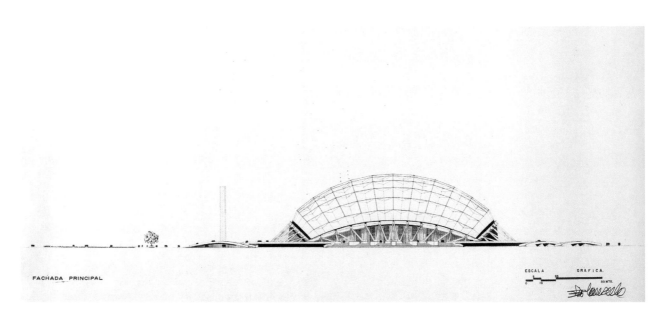

FACHADA PRINCIPAL

ESCALA GRAFICA.
0 10 50 MTS.

Detail of roof

right angles, and the corners are built at a 120-degree angle. All the surfaces are different and covered with hyperbolic paraboloids." This was an unusual way of applying hypars, and it focused on geometric logic because of the problem of the overall differences. Apart from that, while coinciding with Candela's work hypothesis, this type of solution combined the building's structure and aesthetics, since the backs of the copper-covered spherical segments made of hypars stand out as aesthetic elements on the exterior of the structure: a glittering, scaled armor anchored to the ground with V-shaped concrete struts. Candela had no trouble explaining this work: "Here we return to one of my earliest claims, namely that structural design possesses more art than it does science."

Compared to similar projects completed in other countries, the building's final dimensions represented a structure of superlatives for that era. From the curved lattice girders to the maintained clearance, it measured 628 feet in one direction and 436 feet in the other. The structural solution clearly contributes to the building's uniqueness and architectural value. With many of Candela's concrete membranes it was obvious how he gave expression to the building's virtual lightness. Yet this very sensation was reversed in the case of the Olympic Sports Complex, whose structure seemed rooted to the ground with an exceptional force—an impression not only conveyed through the concrete abutments, but equally so through the formal stringency of the brick wall on which the steel dome's framework rested. The geometry of the hypars was perfectly suited to satisfying the metric demands of every space. Still, it was unknown at that moment whether the hypars would be used as fillings or as secondary elements, or even what type of construction to employ for that matter. The design was based on a

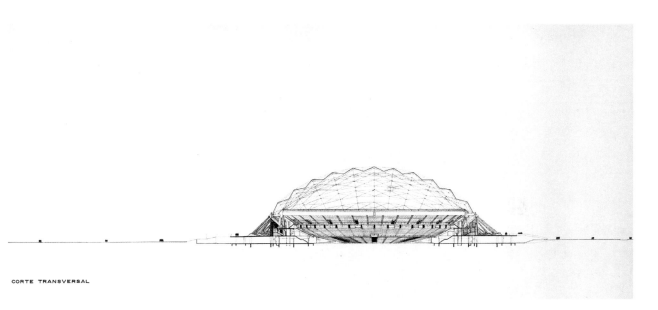

CORTE TRANSVERSAL

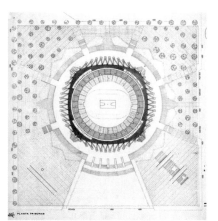

Ground-floor plan

four-cornered grid network with aluminum piping, which served as the foundation for the hypar; followed by a two-layered surfacing of plywood panels with a waterproof coating; and finally the 100 x 400-foot strips of copper sheeting. The result was a glittering roof membrane made of 21,400 square feet of copper sheeting—at its time the world's largest copper roof.

Even today this work remains an exemplary piece of architecture. While celebrating the rational mathematical calculations that underlie its formal stability, the stadium exists in complete accord with the thinking of its creator. Candela excelled in creating buildings in which structure plays a decisive role in the definition of form: far from concealing itself, this reveals itself as an identity-generating element of the stadium and gives expression to its aesthetic quality.

A year after the stadium's success worldwide, Candela's disposition began feeling the effects of the dissatisfying social situation in which he lived. Ultimately, this prompted him to leave Mexico. In a 1969 speech delivered to students of the *Escuela Nacional de Arquitectura* at the UNAM, he said: "[...] I am almost sixty years old, I have spent practically twenty of those years designing and constructing buildings, and I know rather well what it means to work as a conventional architect. Yet I find neither a market nor a use for many of the abilities that it took me years to acquire."

Life and Work

Félix Candela giving a lecture

Opposite page:
Félix Candela, 1956

1910 ▶ Félix Candela is born January 27 in Madrid.

1935 ▶ Acquires degree in Architecture at the *Escuela Superior de Arquitectura de Madrid.* As a student gives fellow classmates private instruction in geometry and tension theories. During this study phase his principal instructor is Professor Luis Vegas, a structural-theory specialist who corrects Candela's uncertain first attempts. In his sixth year of study, Candela's interest in shell construction becomes apparent: Eduardo Torroja constructs the *Frontón de Recoletos,* a work carefully studied by Candela.

1937–1939 ▶ Serves as captain in the Engineering Corps of Spain's Republican Party; interned in a concentration camp in Perpignan; and flees to Mexico, where he arrives as a political refugee in Veracruz.

1940 ▶ Marries Eladia Martín.

1941 ▶ Obtains Mexican citizenship.

1940–1948 ▶ Until 1948 works as a freelance architect and accepts construction-related assignments as coworker or partner of various architects' offices and construction firms.

1949 ▶ Founds the company of *Cubiertas Ala, S. A.* and serves as its president until 1969. Builds with *Cubiertas* and its branches outside Mexico over 896 structures with a regulated surface system (hypars).

1951 ▶ In a memorandum of the *Congreso Científico Mexicano* (Scientific Congress of Mexico) presents the first version of his essay *Toward a New Philosophy of Structures,* later published in book and pamphlet form in Argentina and Mexico.

1951–1952
Cosmic Rays Pavilion, Ciudad Universitaria, Mexico City, in collaboration with the architect Jorge González Reyna

1952
Chemical Sciences Auditorium, Ciudad Universitaria, Mexico City, in collaboration with

the architects Enrique Yáñez, Guillermo Rosell, and Enrique Guerrero

1953 ▶ Begins instructing as professor of Material Science and Tensile Strength at the *Escuela Nacional de Arquitectura* of the UNAM, interrupted by his leaving Mexico in 1970. Publishes the essay *Structural Digressions on Style in Architecture* in *Espacios* magazine, Mexico.

1952–1954
Customs Administration Warehouses, Vallejo Industrial District, Mexico City, in collaboration with the architect Carlos Recamier

1954
La Jacaranda Nightclub, Mexico City, in collaboration with the architect Max Borges, Jr.

1953–1955
Church of Our Miraculous Lady, Narvarte, Mexico City

1955 ▶ At the age of forty-five, at the zenith of his professional career, Candela completes the construction of thirty-one important works in this year alone, a record never broken by another Mexican architect.
Coyoacán Market, Mexico City, in collaboration with the architect Pedro Ramírez Vázquez
Our Lady of Solitude Chapel, El Altillo, Coyoacán, Mexico City, in collaboration with the architects Enrique de la Mora and Fernando López Carmona
Main Hall of Mexico's New Stock Exchange, Mexico City, in collaboration with the architects Enrique de la Mora and Fernando López Carmona

1956 ▶ Gives the lecture *In Defense of Formalism* at the *Casa del Arquitecto* (Architectural Association), Mexico City.
Church of Saint Anthony of the Orchards, Mexico City, in collaboration with the architects Enrique de la Mora and Fernando López Carmona
Factory Gate of the Lederle Laboratories, Mexico City, in collaboration with the architect Alejandro Prieto

1957 ▶ Exhibition of his works at the University of Southern California, Los Angeles, USA

Jamaica Wholesale Market, Mexico City
La Jacaranda Nightclub, Acapulco, Guerrero,
in collaboration with the architect Juan Sordo
Madaleno
Entranceway Sculpture at Lomas Tropicales de
Tequesquitengo housing colony, Tequesquitengo,
Morelos, in collaboration with the architects
Guillermo Rosell and Manuel Larrosa

1958
Plaza of the Fans (Plaza Los Abanicos),
Lomas de Cuernavaca, Morelos, in collaboration
with the architects Guillermo Rosell and Manuel
Larrosa
Los Manantiales Restaurant, Xochimilco, Mexico
City, in collaboration with the architects
Fernando and Joaquín Álvarez Ordoñez

1959
Lomas de Cuernavaca Chapel, Cuernavaca,
Morelos, in collaboration with the architects
Guillermo Rosell and Manuel Larrosa
Church of Saint Joseph the Laborer, Monterrey,
Nuevo León, in collaboration with the architects
Enrique de la Mora and Fernando López Carmona

1959–1960
San Vicente de Paul Chapel, Coyoacán, Mexico
City, in collaboration with the architects Enrique
de la Mora and Fernando López Carmona

1960 ▸ Publishes his treatise General Formulas for
Membrane Stresses in Hyperbolic Paraboloidical
Shells in the ACI, considered his most important
paper by Antonio Tondo.
Bacardi & Co. Bottling Plant, Cuautitlán, State of
Mexico, in collaboration with the architects
Saenz-Cancio-Martín-Álvarez and Gutiérrez;
consulting engineer: Luis Torres Landa
Santa Monica Church, Mexico City, in
collaboration with the architect Fernando López
Carmona

1961 ▸ Exhibition of his works at Harvard
University, Cambridge, Massachusetts, USA

1963 ▸ Death of his wife, Eladia, with whom he
has four children: Antonia, Manuela, Teresa, and
Pilar

1966 ▸ Exhibition of his works in the McNair
Museum, San Antonio, Texas, USA, and the
Museum of Modern Art, Houston, Texas, USA
La Florida Church, Naucalpan, State of Mexico

1967 ▸ Marries the North American architect
Dorothy Davies.
Candelaria and San Lázaro subway stations,
Mexico City, the latter based on the design by the
architect Julio Michel Sinner

1968 ▸ Publishes the article The Sydney Opera
House Scandal in Arquitectura México magazine.
Olympic Sports Complex, Mexico City, in
collaboration with the architects Antoni Peyri
and Enrique Castañeda Tamborrel

1969 ▸ Architectural work for Praeger-Kawanagh-
Waterbury, New York, USA

1971 ▸ Emigrates to the United States. From this
year until 1978 professorship in the Architecture
Department at the University of Illinois, Chicago,
Illinois. Works as international consultant for
various architectural firms until the year of his
death.

1975
Estadio Santiago Bernabeu, Madrid, Spain:
Stadium Project

1977 ▸ Works as a consultant for a project of the
King Abdulaziz University, Jiddah, Saudi Arabia,
courtesy of the Project Planning Association,
Toronto, Canada.

1978 ▸ Obtains US citizenship.

1980 ▸ Works as a freelance specialized
consultant in Madrid.

1994 ▸ Spanish government organizes a
retrospective of Candela's life and work in Madrid.

1997 ▸ Candela dies on December 7 of a long-
existing cardiac insufficiency, in Durham, Raleigh,
North Carolina, USA.

**Félix Candela using a model to explain the
structural analysis of a roof shell**

México

Bibliography

Credits

The Author

▶ Basterra and E. Valero: "La aventura mexicana: Entre-vista con Félix Candela," in *Arquitectura Viva*, Madrid, No. 58, January-February 1998, pp. 75-77
▶ Buschiazzo, Félix E.: *Félix Candela*, 1st edition, Buenos Aires, Instituto de Arte Americano e Investigaciones Estéticas, 1961, p. 56
▶ Candela, Félix: "Two New Churches in Mexico," in *In Defense of Formalism and Other Writings*, 1st edition, Bilbao, Xarait Ediciones, 1989, pp. 21-30
▶ Candela, Félix: "Structural Digressions on Style in Architecture," ibid., pp. 31-40
▶ Candela, Félix: "Encuesta de la revista Espacios," ibid., pp. 41-50
▶ Candela, Félix: "La iglesia de la Virgen Milagrosa," ibid., pp. 51-56
▶ Candela, Félix: "The Sydney Opera House Scandal," ibid., pp. 57-64
▶ Candela, Félix: "Encuesta de la revista Arquitectura de México," ibid., pp. 65-72
▶ Candela, Félix: "Toward a New Philosophy of Structures," ibid., pp. 73-88
▶ Cervera, Jaime: "Un genio al margen: Félix Candela, 1910-1997," in *Arquitectura Viva*, Madrid, No. 58, January-February, 1998, pp. 72-74
▶ Faber, Colin: *Candela: The Shell Builder*, 1st edition, New York, Reinhold Publishing Corporation, 1963, p. 240
▶ Rivera, Héctor, "Estoy contento de haber logrado que México suene en el mundo de la arquitectura," in *Proceso*, Mexico, No. 892, December 6, 1993, pp. 48-51
▶ Smith, Clive Bamford: *Builders in the Sun: Five Mexican Architects*, special edition, New York, Architectural Book Publishing Co. Inc., 1967, p. 224ff.
▶ Tonda, Juan Antonio, *Félix Candela*, 1st edition, Mexico, Consejo Nacional para la Cultura y las Artes, "Círculo de Arte", 2000, p. 32
▶ "Comentarios," in *Calli* magazine, Mexico, No. 35, 1968, pp. 30-33
▶ *Félix Candela: Arquitecto*, 1st edition, catalog to the exhibition organized by the Instituto Juan de Herrera and the Department for Housing, Urban Planning and Architecture of the Ministry of Public Works, Transport and Environment, Madrid, 1994, p. 176
▶ "Félix Candela, Biographical Data," in *Calli* magazine, Mexico, No. 33, May-June 1968, pp. 25-29
▶ Interview with Félix Candela, conducted by Enrique X. de Anda Alanís on November 25, 1989, Mexico City

Born in Mexico City, Enrique X. de Anda Alanís is an architect who received a doctorate in Art History at the Universidad Nacional Autónoma de México (UNAM). He studied the history of modern art in Mexico at the Instituto de Investigaciones Estéticas of the UNAM and is the author of seven books as well as co-author of an additional seventeen publications, all of which address the art and architecture of modernism. His work has been awarded seven national prizes, including two from the Instituto Nacional de Antropología e Historia de México and one from the UNAM. A Getty Foundation grant recipient, he has curated exhibitions on Art Nouveau and Art Déco. His lecture tours have taken him to Latin America, the United States, Spain, and Australia. He is a member of the Academía Nacional de Arquitectura de México and co-president of the Comité Internacional de Arquitectura del Siglo XX de ICOMOS Internacional, an institution dedicated to the preservation of cultural inheritance.